The Promise of

Lilacs

An inspirational story
of courage and empowerment

LEAH ALMARIO-RIVERA

Disclaimer

This book is a memoir, my personal story. I have
tried to recreate events, locales, and conversations
from my recollection of them.
I have changed the name of some individuals and
places, compressed some events, and rephrased some
dialogues to
maintain their anonymity.

For my son, Gordon.
For my mama, Thelma.

CONTENTS

FOREWORD

Early in my career as a registered speech-language pathologist (SLP) and budding behavior analyst working with families of children diagnosed on the autism spectrum, it was apparent that these families had as much to teach me—about the human spirit and dedication to achieving the best outcomes for their child—as I did to teach them about the uniqueness of their child, the evidence for treatments they may be exploring, and the necessary effort required to see progress and for maximum independence and quality of life. I was a somewhat seasoned professional at the time I had the pleasure of meeting Leah, Bingo, and Gordon. However, at that time their commitment to providing their son with what he required amazed me as both a speech pathologist and a fairly new mother. In the subsequent years since first meeting the Riveras, the application and outcomes associated with using Applied Behavior Analysis (ABA) as part of a treatment package for children with autism spectrum disorders (ASD) served to further convince me that ABA was a necessary ingredient for many children with ASD to gain the requisite skills needed to participate and succeed in life. As well, it could help parents to learn effective, efficient strategies and the means for analyzing the immediate environment to make the behavior changes required to handle the challenges that would come their way. Currently, as both an SLP and a Board Certified Behavior Analyst (BCBA), this book is a great reminder to me of the gifts we can impart to families and clients and of the part each of us play in their journey; additionally, it can remind us as professionals of the overall impact of the work, decisions, stressors, and losses that each family encounters along their journey.

Leah has written this story with her heart. It is a unique and detailed look into one family's journey through marriage, emigrating to another country, the birth of their children, receiving a difficult diagnosis, and a look forward into the future. Their story is raw and factual yet demonstrates the struggles that are very real for many families who are diverted off their current path to a very different one which includes welcoming many strangers into their lives to assist them in the care of their child. This excursion is often one of "one step forward, two steps back,"—oftentimes with the goal being somewhat elusive and not a sure thing.

The chronicle begins on Mother's Day in 1997 and ends exactly twenty-two years later, in May of 2019. Leah recollects many details at each important stage of Gordon's life. The birth is joyful but takes a somber turn as those important childhood stages are missed. A look through the toddler years highlights the quest for information along with solicitation of advice and hoping for confirmation from friends and acquaintances that what you are seeing isn't serious (despite what your maternal instincts are telling you!) as she writes, "Is his behavior normal, a phase? Or was this symptomatic of something?" Leah honestly describes the interactions with various professionals such as the child psychiatrist who delivers the diagnosis, "With little introduction, he delivers his diagnosis: 'Gordon has autism.' and then confirms it when further questioned, 'That's what I said. He has autism.' He reiterates, nonchalantly, like he has delivered this diagnosis a thousand times." These scenarios are important reminders for everyone working with families. Even though our jobs are our norm, and we go through these same activities with high frequency, the families we work with do not. Empathy, compassion, and humility are qualities which should be prerequisites for anyone working with individuals who have challenges of any type.

Leah continues through their journey toward finding the 'right' therapy or combination of therapies. Not dissimilar to thousands upon thousands of families in similar situations, this was a trial and error approach. Twenty-years ago, a diagnosis of ASD was somewhat of a rarity with only about 1 in 2,500 births resulting in that diagnosis. At that time, treatment options were limited; the internet was just beginning to become a repository for information and a manner to connect with others, and knowledgeable professionals to aid in treatment navigation were few and far between. Fast forward twenty years and there have been some notable changes in incidence, treatment evidence, and access to information. However, navigating healthcare systems, weeding out pseudoscience from empirically supported treatments, and the demands on the entire family have continued and, in some cases, increased in complexity and magnitude. Leah continues to write about their journey through ineffective treatments, treatments that were consultative in nature at best. "I have here some ideas for promoting speech." She takes a sheet of paper with a list of suggestions from the stack of files and hands them to me. "And I'd like to see him every six to eight weeks." She also describes their foray into the school system with a child who was "still non-verbal and not toilet-trained."

Eventually, the Riveras returned to see the child psychiatrist, hopeful that there had been positive changes. Once again, they were crushed and downtrodden when they heard, "This isn't rocket science. Your son is autistic." On the contrary, it is akin to rocket science. Parents must immerse themselves in foreign studies in scientific fields and grapple with knowledge translation and application to assist their children. These are not easy times. Leah forges on despite the blows dealt to her and to Gordon, and a review of her life, Gordon's development, and the unknown years ahead becomes an annual ritual on each Mother's Day. Leah continued to explore any treatment offered and soon stumbled upon applied behavior analysis. Bingo recounted a newspaper article about Dr. Ivar Lovaas from UCLA, reading aloud to Leah, "It's true and is effective. Dr. Lovaas helps to popularize this approach and performed his own experiment where those who were subjected to a one-on-one therapy over forty hours per week made significant developmental gains within a few months." Soon Leah would be running and managing a home ABA program with the help of new friends and eager young therapists. It became her second full-time job. The more skills Gordon displayed, the more Leah became immersed in his ABA therapy with a renewed sense of purpose, hope, and determination. It became a way of life, and her ability to analyze all situations—no matter the context—assisted Gordon and those around her to adapt their teaching, the environment, and the targets to where Gordon was currently functioning and where he needed to get to.

With the implementation of effective treatments such as ABA, the Picture Exchange Communication System (PECS), the school as a collaborative (although not always willing) partner, Gordon began to make significant progress. Communication is behavior that involves both a speaker and a listener/audience. It brings the entire family together as witnessed through Leah's recounting at the beginning of PECS implementation. "With Patrick's assistance, Gordon attaches the picture to the same sentence strip and hands over the sentence strip to Bingo. We all watch in awe of the progress he has made. My heart leaps. That's my boy! "Bacon." Bingo beams. "Here you go, bacon." Then he gives Gordon the bacon. A big smile plays in Gordon's lips as he gobbles a piece. I take a huge bite of bacon, letting the taste linger in my mouth, realizing that breakfast with the family is now starting to feel normal."

As Gordon developed and aged, Leah and her husband found a sense of community and shared experience in some support groups that they joined. Those groups became the family that they didn't have surrounding them, propping them up when needed, giving them much needed respite without judgment, and paving the way for other experiences that would have a significant and profoundly lasting effect on Gordon and his entire family. Through the behavioral difficulties and outbursts which led to feelings of exhaustion, shame, and guilt, the Riveras rose to each occasion and showed a resilience that many would crumble under if given the same circumstances. These families are relentless in the fight for what their children need. Even when the other siblings leave the nest to succeed on their own, parents of children with disabilities put aside their own needs, aspirations, and typical thoughts of the future—traveling, retirement, slowing down—to care for their adult children. It is not the typical path, but on it there is still joy, work, community, growth, and love.

None of us know from the beginning of the journey what the future holds at the end. For some families, the hard work, dedication, and effort results in significant (and sometimes almost miraculous) results, yet for others, even with the same hard work, dedication, and effort, the results might be less than "ideal" but still significant for that individual (and their family). Leah reminds all of us that if you don't put the time and effort in, right from the beginning, then living with the 'what ifs' could become debilitating for you and for your child.

This book is a necessary reminder of the 'jagged journey' that parents take in order to ensure that their child reaches their potential. On the other hand, it is also a stark reminder of the role that others along the path may play. There are those who have a chance to contribute to the future potential or, if unaware of their impact, may throw stumbling blocks in the way, hinder the untapped potential, and increase the parents' stress.

It's an important read for parents of children with ASD of all ages as well as for any professional, from a new clinician to a seasoned one, of the importance of empathy, humility, and compassion while being the navigator that these families require.

Tracie L. Lindblad, M.Sc., Reg. SLP, M.Ed., BCBA
Speech-Language Pathologist, Board Certified Behavior Analyst
Clinical Director, Monarch House
Adjunct Lecturer, University of Toronto
Oakville, Ontario Canada, 2019

"Parenthood is about raising and celebrating the child you have, not the child you thought you'd have.

It's about understanding your child is exactly the person they are supposed to be.

And, if you're lucky, they might be the teacher who

turns you into the person you're supposed to be."

– Joan Ryan, *Water Giver*

ONE

"Within every child is a connection to one form or another and a potential waiting to be fulfilled."

– Dr. Stephen Mark Shore

May 1997

The sweet, powerful fragrance of lilacs wafted through the air as I stirred honey into my cup of chamomile tea. The burst of the pink-hued lilacs in bloom outside my kitchen this spring convinced me that everything would be all right. What a lie. I sipped my tea, pleasantly surprised that it didn't burn my mouth.

The cool breeze brushed against my skin, taking me back to the memory of the wintry January this year when my son, Gordon, then three years and three months old, was diagnosed with autism. Although my suspicions had been brewing for the past year and a half, I still couldn't fathom this diagnosis. The word *autism* sounded far-fetched. Yet, the reality of my son's condition led me to engage in the ramifications of this new life for me and my family.

His play was strange to me. I was baffled as I noticed him enthralled while pushing his tiny Matchbox car back and forth on the kitchen table. *I was mesmerized.* His deep-set eyes were intense as they focused on his play. A tiny grin melted my heart. I sighed, wishing he would stop for one moment and just looked at me. Yet, here I was, watching his toy car's relentless journey to nowhere, which hypnotized me. *He looked happy and content in his own world, I reminded myself.* I often wondered if Gordon knew that something was not right. Running my fingers through his hair, I stole a kiss and whispered, "I love you, sweetie."

He inched backward and stared at his car, oblivious of my presence in his midst. At three years old, he had not said a word and wasn't potty-trained yet. He had not uttered any sound that resembled that syllable for mom, or dad, or any intelligible word. He was an expert at pushing his little car back and forth in a precise line within six inches long for hours at a time. This exercise didn't elicit a smile or any comprehensible sound other than the repetitive "ba-ba-ba" he'd been uttering since he was ten months old, an incessant babbling. I often tried to comprehend what fascinated him with this routine, occupying him for endless hours. Was it the repetitive motion that offered solace?

As a mother of a child with autism, I wished I could understand how he thinks, why he did what he did, and how I could enter his world...but it was indeed more than that. I wanted him to know how much I loved him.

I grabbed a similar toy car and followed what he did to get his attention.

"Ba-ba-ba," I imitated him. He ignored me. I inched closer to him. "You're my sweetheart. You know Mommy loves you, right?"

Without a word or a fuss, Gordon moved farther away from me and carried on with his act. I scooted closer to him, trying to maintain eye contact, but he ignored me, headed to the family room, and continued his play on top of the coffee table. I buried the toy car inside my pocket and sighed. Tears spilled from my eyes. I yanked my mug, hoping the warmth of the tea could ease the creepy sensation inside me, but it's now cold, reminding me of that same feeling I had when the doctor first uttered my son's autism diagnosis.

Gordon was here, and he wasn't here at the same time. Gordon's focal points in the universe were cars, cars, cars—not his mother, not his father, not his brother… no human being. If he needed water, he climbed up on the counter, grabbed a glass from the cupboard, opened the fridge, and helped himself. If there was no glass within reach, he didn't ask for help. He would rather go thirsty or hungry than involve someone's aid. He couldn't speak or point or gesture, so it was easier for him to do what he could do alone to satisfy his needs. Confounded, I didn't understand why he didn't involve us in simple tasks.

"Yoo-hoo, Mom's here!" I chirped, waving to capture his attention, but he continued to ignore me. *Was I a ghost to him*? As I realized my bucket full of emotions was spilling over, I noticed I was gripping my teacup with white knuckles. Wishing to ease my frustrations, I diverted my gaze to the window above the countertop. My eyes rested on the lilac bushes with intense pink flowers, framed with lush green leaves and two maple trees in the background. As I savored the lilac scent floating through my kitchen, I was comforted for a moment by the light breeze. I wished this moment could last forever so I could erase any thought of the doctor's news, obliterating the fact that Gordon had autism.

Then it hit me, and I was reminded that it was Mother's Day, and I hoped Gordon knew I was his mother. Flowers in bloom reminded me that spring was here: a season of rebirth and new beginnings. *Would Gordon call me Mom soon?*

TWO

"Stop worrying about the world ending today.
It's already tomorrow in Australia."

– Charles Monroe Schulz

May 1997

When we first set foot in Canada nine years ago, the same year we got married in 1988, we looked forward to our new life in this foreign land. Canada offered exciting opportunities. During our sleepless nights, we convinced ourselves that we made the right move despite being thousands of miles away from our families.

With Bingo's work experience, an MBA in finance, and my work experience in computer systems, life looked promising. In my field, jobs were abundant. I found employment at once.

Bingo didn't share the same fate, yet he never gave up his search. While I was at work, he spent his day at the public library, checking the newspapers for job postings in the mornings and submitting his applications before the day ended. On days when there was no job posting to respond to, he'd read books and journals to enrich his Canadian knowledge.

One chilly winter evening as we gathered at the dinner table, Bingo's eyes widened. "Guess what I learned today?"

As I sliced a piece of chicken adobo, which I simmered in native vinegar the night before, I smiled. "Tell me."

"Are you aware that the longest street in the world is Yonge Street, the one in downtown Toronto?" With arched eyebrows and hands in motion, he quizzed me. This reminded me of his enthusiasm when we first met during our college days. As a campus leader, I realized then that my husband was always passionate about pursuing his dreams despite the circumstances and resilience in overcoming challenges. I admired his tenacity in everything he set his eyes on.

"Are you kidding me?" I raised my eyebrows, fascinated by this tidbit.

"Seriously, it goes north, then it curves toward Minnesota, without a name change." He took a sip of water before continuing. "And do you know that Oakville is the most populous town in Canada?"

"Oh, neat! And why is this not a city? Why has Oakville remained a town? I bet the Guinness Book of Records has that fact." I always looked forward to dinnertime when Bingo shared his latest tidbits of Canadian knowledge. I found those facts interesting.

A few weeks after Bingo had sent out the application letters, rejections started coming in. Despite his educational achievements and accomplishments, the managers in finance were only interested in hiring those applicants with Canadian experience. Was there a difference between Canadian and Philippine finance? The elements of finance and math are universal, I thought. It made little sense, but it was their policy.

"What happens if I don't get a job?" He asked with a frown creasing his forehead when we learned I was pregnant. As unemployment dragged on into its sixth month, Bingo no longer shared any Canadian fun facts.

Upon reaching home from work, Bingo was in our bedroom watching basketball on TV with a blank stare. At the time, we were renting a master bedroom of a semi-detached home in Oakville. All our belongings, the queen-sized bed, the chest of drawers, a TV, and our wedding portrait were in that room.

Glancing at our wedding portrait, I could see my groom's bright smile as if he had just won an award.

My forced smile revealed the wedding jitters I had before walking down the aisle. Deep inside me, I knew we would build a life together, in sickness or in health, in richness or in poor, till death do we part.

A chill came tingling down my spine as I realized that both positive and negative changes would leave me fidgety. Pushing away my thoughts, I reminded myself I needed to be strong for Bingo, for us and our future.

"How was your day?" I set the keys on the night table, removed my pumps, and dragged my feet on the taupe carpet, glad to be home after a hectic day at work.

His eyes look guarded, and I could sense something was wrong. We learned I was pregnant the day before, and there seemed to be a distance between us.

Approaching him, I grasped the remote control and turned the TV off.

"Hey? What was that for?"

Leaning forward, I pressed my lips on his and gave him a tight embrace. "We need to talk."

He heaved a sigh. With his fingers interlocked, he blurted out, "How am I supposed to feed our baby?"

"Bingo." I comforted him while clasping his hands tight. "Don't worry about it. We haven't been in Canada for a year yet."

"But it's been six months," he said with a resigned tone.

He was right, and what if he couldn't find a job? A thud roared in my chest. "Do you think we should move back to the Philippines?"

Unsure if this was an option, I wanted him to know that no matter what he decided, I would support him. It would be our decision. "Perhaps we can move a month after I give birth."

Bingo didn't say a word, and I left it at that, not wanting our emotions to rule our decision.

***

Patience and determination finally paid off. Bingo got not only one job, but two. One was delivering papers at 4:00 a.m. for the Toronto Star, and then later in the day, he worked as a teller with Canada Trust Bank. He continued to send out resumes at night, folding them and licking stamps until late in the evening when he would fall asleep in our big faux leather chair with several unstamped envelopes sitting on his chest.

During his first day of work at the bank, Bingo set his briefcase on the counter and straightened his shoulders.

A tall Caucasian man reached out and offered him a handshake. "Good morning, I'm George. I sit right beside you."

Bingo looked at him in the eye and extended a firm grip. "Mesiton, pleased to meet you."

"Did you say Messon or Mestion?"

"Me-si-ton." He repeated his name, emphasizing each syllable, in case his accent sounded foreign to the gentleman.

George raised his eyebrows, then nodded shortly after.

"Okay, just call me 'Bingo.'" He suggested to be called by his nickname, when it seemed that no could pronounce his name properly.

"Oh, Bingo!" Everyone cheered, amused with his nickname. Quickly, everyone joined in chorus, singing that famous children's song, *and Bingo was his name-o.* Given all the confusion over his real name, he didn't want to further complicate things and start off on the wrong foot, so Bingo didn't bother to explain his nickname and just sang along with them, because more than anything, he was glad to have a job.

***

By the time I gave birth to Patrick in January of the following year, Bingo got a job with the Royal Bank of Canada in the field more aligned to his work experience in the Philippines.

"Will you take time off work?" I asked him the day after I gave birth while I was still in the hospital.

"I can't, remember? I just got this job two months ago. I still have to prove myself." He smiled at me while stroking my hair. "Listen, I'll be here as soon as you are discharged."

I let the tears run down my cheeks when he left for work that day. Outside the window, I saw snowflakes coming down. My body felt cold. For the first time since stepping onto this Canadian soil two years ago, I missed home. I missed my mother, who promised to come when I gave birth. Work priorities got in the way which made her cancel her plans at the last minute.

"It's feeding time." The nurse's announcement interrupted my thoughts. In her uniform of pink pants and blouse scrub, she handed me my baby wrapped in a flannel blue-and-white blanket. "Are you expecting any visitors?"

"No. No visitors," I responded in a resigned tone.

"Smile, be happy." She cheered me up as she adjusted my arms, showing me the breast- feeding position and propping a pillow under my elbow. "Do you know that your baby can sense your emotions?"

I looked up at her, puzzled. I focused my thoughts on this new skill, how to breastfeed my baby. *I wish my mother was here.* For sure, she was surrounded by family and friends when she gave birth to her first-born. In my case, I left the country of my own will. Had my mother made it here, that would be a bonus, I remind myself, but it was not to be expected.

I knew in due time Bingo would be there for me and for our family. I believed in us.

THREE

"Your siblings are the only people in the world who know what it's like to have been brought up the way you were."

– Betsy Cohen

January 1997

As we meandered our way through the halls of the Credit Valley Hospital in Mississauga, I couldn't help but admire the interior architecture of this hospital—the newest hospital in the province. Inside this building, the thoughts of the worst-case scenario lingered in my mind as I tried to ignore that something inside me that kept on quivering. The inviting atrium that resembled a lobby of a grand hotel or an art museum had momentarily eased those pangs.

"Who did you say are we seeing at this hospital?" Bingo nudged my arm to remind me we were there for a specific purpose. In his office attire—black pants and a plain white shirt—he planned to head to work after that visit. Gordon clung to Bingo's hands, while his mittens dangled outside his coat sleeves.

"There's a lot of natural light in here. Don't you just love this, Bingo?" I shared my thoughts with him. I admired the graceful exposed wooden beams arching from ceiling to floor, the *ficus benjamina* tree and other greeneries, non-white leather seats, and so much more. The ambiance led me to forget for a moment I was at a hospital. On this chilly, snowy morning, there was nothing more soothing than feeling the warmth of the sun.

"Leah." Bingo faced me with his signature arched eyebrows. "Did you hear me?"

That tone meant to *hurry*. I heard him, but I was also savoring the ambiance of that place. How I wished I could just stay there while I watched the passersby and savored the moment. "Coming." I trailed behind him, taking one last look at the atrium.

Sometimes, I wished Bingo would slow down and smell the roses, as the cliché goes. Why did everything have to be purposeful for him?

"Relax, my dear," I teased him, in my effort to have him recognize and enjoy the atmosphere as I saw it. Were other men like him? Did they always see things in black or white and not a gray in their horizon? Whatever reason, God must have had a purpose for bringing us together.

"Don't you love this place? Why didn't I give birth here?" My sons were born in Mississauga but not at that hospital.

He rolled his eyes, noticing how slow I walked. I chuckled to myself. If I could have just read his thoughts, he must have been screaming at me, "Women!"

I strode rapidly, reminding myself that we had an appointment, the appointment we'd been waiting for since last October. But by then, this doctor had closed his doors and stopped seeing patients for the rest of the year, having reached his annual doctor's income, capped by the Ontario Ministry of Health.

We approached the elevator to check the listing of the professionals working in that hospital. I ran my fingers through the list.

"There." I pointed to the name. "Pelletier, Leon, Child Psychiatrist. We're seeing him. That way, then."

Dr. Pelletier's office waiting area was nothing like the atrium. A chair rail divided the wall with mint green on top and ivory on the bottom portion. I wondered if someone plucked that office from one hospital and dropped it in there because the disparity was clear and didn't belong to that hospital. *A man's office, for sure.* Eight chairs with white thin pads lined the walls. Piles of *Psychiatry Today* and other parent magazines were neatly piled on the center of the glass coffee table. Children's toys were in one corner of the waiting room.

I wished they had some bright colors to make this place more uplifting. Nonetheless, Bingo and I were relieved to be here with Gordon, three years and three months old, hoping we could sort this out.

My thoughts shifted to how that all began. Our main concern was that Gordon bore no coherent language. We had been insisting Dr. Bell, our family doctor, for some referrals. When Gordon was two years old, he referred us to the audiologist.

"His hearing is perfect," the audiologist declared.

"Are you sure?" Part of me wished that hearing was the reason he had no words yet. "How about the pitch? The tone?" I argued as if I knew the attributes of sound.

"Nothing's amiss," the audiologist confirmed his findings.

At two and a half years old, Dr. Bell encouraged us not to worry and reminded us that Patrick first started talking when he was almost three years old. Although he assured us that each delay seemed to be normal because Gordon was meeting his developmental milestones, I could sense something was wrong.

Maybe I was just paranoid. It didn't help that Bingo thought I speculated a lot and jumped into conclusions right away. Perhaps there was nothing wrong with Gordon, I would pacify myself after each visit with Dr. Bell. Each child developed at their own pace. I reminded myself that Gordon first drank from the glass at one year old during our visit to New Jersey. On this regard, he was ahead of Patrick who was finally weaned off the baby bottle at three years old. As my sister would say, "Yeah, these younger siblings pick up quick. They have their older brother to imitate."

In one of my phone calls to the family, I shared with my brother, Vittorio, that Gordon was so occupied with cars all day. "Why is he like that? Why can't he run those cars on that rug with the road map?"

"I can relate to that," he said. "Finally. Somebody in the family is like me."

"What do you mean?" I asked, piqued with curiosity.

"When I was young," he said, as he started to share with me his childhood story I've heard a million times before. "I could never understand those boys' games, running around, or playing with marbles. Why can't they just play with cars or draw cars?"

Okay, so maybe, Gordon was like Vittorio. Hope surfaced from the inside.

Gordon's first babysitter, who had looked after him since he was six months old, considered herself fortunate to be looking after my son. He was gregarious and funny but never fuzzy. To her delight, she could leave him alone in the playpen. He seemed to entertain himself at two years old.

When his babysitter left town in the fall of 1996, we had to find another person to take care of Gordon. As luck would have it, Karen, a mother of two children, who lived in our townhome complex, had room for my boys. Her older child, Andrew, who is Gordon's age, was quite a chatty kid and loved to hang out with Patrick before Patrick would go to school.

"Are you in a hurry?" Karen greeted me one afternoon when I picked up the boys.

"Nah. What's up? How were my boys today?"

"Come in." She led me to the breakfast nook. "Oh, I love your boys. Andrew and Patrick get along well. Can I offer you some tea?"

"Water is fine, thank you."

As we sat across from each other, Karen told me her story. "We went to the park this morning at our usual time. The usual moms and nannies were there with their children. One mom, Angela, was observing Gordon. She thinks Gordon might have autism. Have you ever thought of that?" She paused, noticing her abruptness. "I'm sorry to spill that on you like that."

I swallowed hard. A thud roared in my chest. "Oh no. That's all right. To be honest, Karen, I've been sensing something is odd with the way he does things. You're the first one who has brought this up." My anxiety led to gratitude, reminding me to trust my instincts. "Thank you for pointing this out. What do you know about autism?"

"Not much. All I know is that they don't want to be hugged. But Gordon is so lovable. I would never have thought he'd have autism."

I thanked Karen and phoned my sister, Cynthia, when I got home. As a registered nurse in New Jersey, I presumed she may have some sense about Gordon's behaviors since she was just here last month.

"Hi, Cynthia." I didn't beat around the bush. "My sitter thinks Gordon has autism. What do you think?"

"Hmm," she responded with some hesitation. "I thought about that. But autistic kids don't want to be near people. They stay away, Leah. They avoid people. They stay in some corner. Gordon's not like that." My head spun. *Is his behavior normal, a phase? Or was this symptomatic of something?*

Cynthia continued. "Now that you've mentioned it, maybe there's something there. I don't know... go have him checked."

I bit my lips. Heat flushed through my body as I wondered if I was not the only one who was noticing the signs. "I've done that, yet my doctor insists there's nothing to worry about."

"No, no, no. Insist on a referral. Family doctors and pediatricians don't diagnose these conditions. Psychiatrists do. You have the right to insist."

Relieved that she was on my side, I assured Cynthia that I would do that right away.

"Don't delay, okay?" She reminded me.

"Not this time. Thank you." I responded in a resigned and helpless tone.

"Mrs. Rivera?" The doctor's receptionist intruded on my thoughts, and I realized that we were at the doctor's office, and I wished I had come earlier. *Why didn't I?*

I approached the reception area.

"Do you have Gordon's health card?" she asked. After handing her the card, she handed me a clipboard and requested me to sign the forms.

Once that was done, I stepped inside the doctor's office.

I studied Dr. Pelletier's office which seemed more businesslike, except for a tiny play area in one corner and an examining table on the other side. Hanging on the wall were his credentials, a graduate of McGill University, his board certification in medicine, another certification in child psychiatry, and much more.

Dressed in a white lab coat, Dr. Pelletier extended his right hand as he greeted us with a warm smile. In his French accent, he asked us many questions, Bingo's and my family histories, my pregnancy, Patrick's early childhood, then Gordon's early childhood. Then Dr. Pelletier led Gordon to the play area. Gordon squatted on the floor while Dr. Pelletier sat on a foot rest stool. With his elbows on his knees, he bent and showed Gordon three stackable rings of different colors. He made sounds and handed them to Gordon. Still, these attempts did not elicit any response nor interest.

"Gordon," he called out his name as he lowered his head to be at his eye level.

No response. Gordon babbled while circling his wrist in a repetitive motion up in the air.

"Look, Gordon." He tried again but this time, with a commanding tone, as he fixed his gaze on his eyes.

No response. It was as if he was a ghost to Gordon.

Chill ran down my spine. *We have been like ghosts to him too.*

Without a word, right in front of Gordon, he stacked the rings one on top of the other, with the largest ring at the bottom, like a kid proceeding to play on his own when his playmate ignores him.

Before he could pile all the rings together, Gordon grabbed one of them and spun it like a steering wheel, accompanied by his babbling.

There he went again with his kind of play. Bingo and I exchanged glances, unsure of what to make out of Gordon's words.

Like the two of them were playing, the doctor tried to engage with Gordon. But as we saw, like what he did at home, Gordon ignored him.

Dr. Pelletier rose from the stool and settled on his leather chair. With little introduction, he delivered his diagnosis: "Gordon has autism."

Although we had already heard this possibility from Karen, hearing the diagnosis from a professional made it official, like a dry seal on a document that cannot be obliterated. I felt like a truck had run over me and ripped my heart to pieces. *Was this for real?* I gripped Bingo's hands, but I couldn't look him in his eyes. *How could this be happening?*

"What do you mean?" I spoke in a hushed tone, hoping he took back what he just said. "Is this official?"

"That's what I said. He has autism," he reiterated nonchalantly, like he had delivered that diagnosis a thousand times. How many parents had he told that their child had autism? How could he just blurt it out that way and not think of the repercussions? That was my son he was talking about. Gordon didn't deserve to have autism.

I glanced at Bingo who now had beads of moisture trickling down his nape.

"Are there any other tests that my son can undergo?" Bingo managed to maintain a straight face, but I could tell, he was in disbelief.

"He doesn't even respond to his name. What other proof will you need?"

I heaved a sigh. His intonation was unsettling.

"I mean, isn't there some kind of blood test?" Bingo's voice quivered. He cleared the lump in his throat. Bingo and I, being mathematics majors, believed that every theory should end with supported hard proof. Reading his mind, I assumed Bingo must think one cannot just diagnose without some blood test or any kind of physiological testing.

"Nope," came his curt response.

"Okay, I hear you, Dr, Pelletier," I interrupted, knowing there was no way we could convince him to say otherwise. "How severe is his autism? Will Gordon overcome this diagnosis?"

"I can confirm that he has severe, classic autism." His lips formed a thin line. "I haven't heard of anyone getting out of it, but nothing is impossible." He shrugged. I puckered my lips and squinted my eyes as

I felt my brain stumbled in a search for words. I stared at my son happily playing his usual repetitive activity.

"And what do you suggest we do?" I was desperate, desperate to find answers and a remedy, desperate that Gordon would overcome his condition. I closed my eyes, trying to find clarity from all of it.

He endorsed a prescription of therapies and added, "And it's best that Gordon goes to an established daycare versus a private babysitter. That way, there are more children he could interact with."

He also requested to see Gordon each year to record the developments.

We were at a loss for words and fumbled as we left the doctor's office. We dashed back to the parking garage akin to having a tunnel vision and a mission to get into the car without delay. *I forgot how much I admired their atrium earlier.*

Bingo didn't say a word on the way home, and I was more worried about the unspoken words. I propped Gordon in his booster seat as he watched in glee the traffic slow down while drivers gave road priority to the snowplows clearing our paths.

"Something's changed." I broke the stillness of our drive, recalling a memory. "Perla cut Gordon's hair when he turned one, and now, he refuses to have his hair touched by anybody."

"I don't know what to say, Leah." Bingo was not in the mood for a conversation. It was difficult for both of us to say the word *autism* and to admit that our son was anything other than normal. But define normal? Who establishes standards? Just because the doctor diagnosed Gordon with autism didn't mean it was real. Or was it?

Scenes of Gordon's early days replayed in my mind as I tried to grasp the moment when things changed. I had always known something wasn't right. I wished I insisted Dr. Bell provide a second opinion or a refer us to a specialist. *I hated that health system; I hated those doctors.*

FOUR

"Do not fear people with Autism, embrace them.
Do not spite people with Autism, unite them. Do
not deny people with Autism, accept them, for
then their abilities will shine."

– Paul Isaacs

March 1997

I n our townhome, our kitchen opened to a breakfast nook with a window that allowed us to view
our little front yard. At the center of this breakfast nook was an oak table which, when extended, accommodated six. With just the four of us, we
served our meals in our breakfast nook. We reserved
the dining room to accommodate more guests. That

kitchen/ breakfast nook area was the heart of our home. Last-minute reminders and news of the day happened there. Good morning kisses, goodbye kisses, hello kisses, and see you later kisses were witnessed there.

I'd always remember the first evening after receiving the news of Gordon's diagnosis. We set foot in our own home like we just came from a funeral and all our out-of-towner guests had left town. So much to do, yet we didn't know what to do.

At dinner that night, Bingo and I just picked at our food with no emotion, even though they were our favorite dishes of baked chicken, rice, string beans, plus fresh lemonade.

The stillness of that evening was unnerving, and however hard I tried to conceal my *emotions in front of my family,* the diagnosis and its ramifications, whatever they may be, continued to linger in my thoughts.

"Gordon, look at me." Patrick stretched his nostrils and shook his head, his palms open by his temple as he tried to cheer his brother.

"Ba-ba-ba." Gordon seemed like he was scanning the room and avoiding Patrick's gaze.

"Are you okay?" I tapped Bingo's shoulders as he stared blankly at what appeared to be the last spoonful of chicken and rice, with crossed arms and stretched legs. He seemed to have lost his appetite for his favorite dish.

I nudged his shoulder.

"You look tired; are you?" I cautiously asked him for fear he would snap at me.

Shaking his head, he said, "Ah, ah, yeah, I am okay." He continued to stare at his plate as he responded. He didn't turn his head toward me.

"Are you going to finish your food?"

Immediately, he gulped the last spoonful, then handed me the plate. "Here, I am done."

Bingo's mind was difficult to read, even if it had been days after the doctor's visit.

At dinner tonight, I could sense that Bingo was deep in thought. I wondered if Bingo blamed me for not addressing the issue earlier, or if he felt accountable for the issue. For fear that it might turn into a lengthy discussion, I hesitated to ask. Besides, what could we do with what had transpired? Could we put the entire blame on Dr. Bell who had reassured us that the delays were normal? I wondered if we failed as parents. I was embarrassed.

The meager knowledge we had on autism then supported the theory that refrigerator moms—moms who lack maternal warmth—were to be blamed for its instance. Had I not connected with my boys? Where had I gone wrong? Without being explicit, we set up an unspoken rule forbidding ourselves to mention the word *autism* or even *diagnosis* to our friends, family, and even to Patrick. We could not share our predicaments with our circle of friends, immigrants like us, who came to Canada in search of a brighter future. Coming from a third world country such as the Philippines, we regard Canada as our utopia. *We supposed everything was perfect in Canada. That setback could not have happened.*

To those who asked about Gordon, we shrugged and told them he was going through some delays. We referred to Gordon as our son who was *not yet verbal and not yet toilet-trained*, the emphasis on *yet* as we were still snooping around for any physiological tests that could explain the etiology of his behavior. In the meantime, his behavior was giving me more goose-bumps by the day.

"Perhaps you could take the boys out while I tidy up here."

He scanned the TV guide in his head. "Yeah, I might as well do that. After last night's Super Bowl game, there's really nothing much to watch on TV to-night, anyway." He turned around. "Where did Patrick go?" He hollered, "Patrick."

"Yes, Dad."

"Put on your shin and elbow pads. You can go in-line skating outside and help me teach Gordon how to ride his tricycle."

"Yippee." Patrick dashed to get his pads.

"Come on, Gordon. No boy goes through child-hood without learning to ride a bike. But first, you need to learn how to ride your tricycle, okay?" Talking to Gordon was akin to talking to a person in a coma. He heard, no doubt, but he didn't respond. No facial reaction, either.

Between Bingo and I, I think he was more in disbelief that the doctor would not conduct any other test to support his findings. *If he cannot prove it, I will*, must be in his thoughts. He believed that those delays were just a phase. Taking a peek from the kitchen window, I observed Bingo and Patrick trying to teach Gordon to ride the tricycle. *If he learned this, he could learn anything, couldn't he?*

Should I, a mother, who was the comforter, healer, and nurturer, need to argue more? Did I need to seek a second opinion when I'd already witnessed Gordon's developmental delays? How was he supposed to start junior kindergarten this coming fall when he still couldn't communicate with others?

Given Bingo's skepticism, I knew I would have to be the one reaching out to the professionals stated in Dr. Pelletier's prescription. After I did my kitchen chores, I headed over to my bedroom and turned on my desktop computer to search for daycares in our area. I noted the telephone number of the established daycare in our area.

The next day, I confirmed a spot for Gordon at the *YMCA* daycare. The daycare occupied an annex at *St. Marguerite d'Youville* school, where Patrick was attending his Grade 2 studies. *Perfect.*

***

In our breakfast nook, the following morning, Bingo tapped on Patrick's shoulders as he slung his backpack and picked up his lunch bag from the counter.

"Are you ready?" He turned to Patrick then gave me a kiss. "Bye, Mom," he said, using his term of endearment he prefers in front of the boys.

Although I'd heard him say that a thousand times, today felt extra special, and I needed to hear that. After kissing Gordon goodbye, Bingo was off to drop Patrick at the sitter, then he needed to catch his 7:00 am express train to Toronto as was his daily routine.

"Bye, Mom." Patrick turned around to give me a kiss, while I was feeding breakfast to Gordon.

"Don't forget your lunch bag," I reminded him.

"I know, I won't," he grunted. Sometimes I felt I could be overbearing as a mother, but that's how much I loved my kids. I just wanted to make sure nothing was amiss; everything was perfect.

As soon as they left the house, I was all alone to collect my thoughts. Thoughts I'd been wrestling with since Dr. Pelletier's visit.

Guilt showered me as I faced Gordon seated in his high chair, shaking with his head from side to side like a shaken rag doll. *I wasn't alone, but I felt alone when I was with him.* When he wasn't steering or twirling an object, he raised his arm and shook his hand like a pom-pom ball. Though already three and a half years old, Gordon needed to be secured with a belt and the table tray while in his high chair.

I raised the cereal bowl above, pretending like it was an airplane and said, "Here comes the cereal bowl, Gordon Zzzzz." I tried to get his attention and cheer him up.

He continued with his hand activity, having no reaction to the imaginary airplane about to land. As soon as the *airplane* landed on the tray, he grabbed it and fidgeted with it like a steering wheel, accompanied with *ba-ba-ba, da-da-da*. I was already accustomed to that behavior which sounded like a buzz of a nearby electric fan. I didn't know what that babbling meant or implied, nor did I know how to stop it. All I was reminded of was that if that vocalization was a precursor to verbalization, it wasn't happening.

I did the same strategy with the spoon on the tray, and he grabbed it and twirled it rapidly.

After I poured the cereal, Gordon fed himself as quickly as he could.

"Gordon, wait a minute. I need to put in milk." I held his hand to stop him from eating more.

While pouring milk, Gordon clung to my arm like he wanted me to stop, but I ignored him. Shortly after, Gordon thrust the bowl, causing his breakfast to drop on the floor, while milk splattered on my clothes from my waist down.

"What was that all about?" I blurted out. I was floored.

"No more breakfast for you. You're going to the daycare with just the little cereal you had, okay?"

"Ba-ba-ba," he carried on with his babbling accompanied by his repetitive hand twisting, which didn't look like a response to my question. Despite the audiologist's report that his hearing was normal, I sometimes doubted that there was something else. Why was my son oblivious to his surroundings?

I mopped our tiled floor, then dashed upstairs for a change of clothes and nylons too.

***

Toward the end of the 1900s, the Millennium bug, the term for a potential computer system crash bound to happen at the turn of the century, dominated the news. As a systems analyst in 1997, I was contracted to investigate our systems and programs and apply the enhancements and fixes to prevent a meltdown in that company.

Imagining how my workday would be during the fifteen-minute drive to work enabled me to switch thoughts off family mode and turn it on to work mode. I usually prided myself in my ability to do that, but not that day. I couldn't seem to shake that morning's incident, so I planned to phone Bingo. As soon as I arrived at my workplace, I dropped my purse in a drawer. I turned on the computer, checked my mail and other Post-It notes left on my desk in case anything needed my immediate attention. Thanks to the portable walls, I had some privacy, and nobody needed to know what happened that morning.

Bingo answered after one ring. His voice sounded flat and uninterested, but that was really his nature. Even if I told him *the sky was falling*, that news would not make him jump out of his seat. Not right away.

"Listen to this. Something weird happened this morning."

"What is it?" Bingo had been at the office for an hour and a half by that time, so I presumed he was engrossed with work. Inside the bank's trading room where he worked, I knew his mornings could be chaotic.

"Gordon knocked down the bowl of cereal." I then proceeded and replayed the incident to Bingo, blow by blow.

"Perhaps it was the milk?" He was quick to analyze a situation and apply the process of elimination.

"Why would that be the case? All babies drink milk." I fumbled with my pen, scribbling milk with bold letters on a Post-It note.

"Beats me. I'm trying to make sense of all this."

"Hmm, maybe." I gripped the phone. *It felt good to run those things by Bingo. He saw things from a different perspective.*

***

The next morning, the plan was for me to drop Patrick off with the before-school care and Gordon at his daycare. I planned to run an experiment while both Patrick and Gordon were at the breakfast nook.

Patrick watched me prepare breakfast. "I need your help," I told him.

He nodded, eyeing Gordon seated in the high chair, babbling.

"I need you to hold Gordon's arms." I was pointing to his forearm.

"Like this?" He reached out to Gordon's arms, following my cue.

"Yes. Hold him well." I poured the cereal into Gordon's bowl.

"Now, take your hands off."

As soon as Patrick removed his hands, Gordon scooped up some of the dry cereal and plunged it inside his mouth.

Patrick and I exchanged glances.

"Observe what he does while I pour milk."

Patrick again took hold of his brother's arms right before the milk was poured. He let go of his brother's arms, and Gordon shoved the cereal bowl just like he did yesterday.

I hand him a glass of milk, but he did the same thing.

"Mom, he doesn't like milk," Patrick raised his voice.

"When did that happen? You both drank milk since the day you were born."

Bingo was right; Gordon didn't like milk. I faced Gordon. *Why on earth did you suddenly detest milk?* There was no use arguing with someone who couldn't respond. When Bingo had become intolerant to lactose, we scratched milk, cheese, and other dairy items off our grocery list. I snuck cheese when I wasn't with them.

But what was it with milk that Gordon seemed to resist? *That's what I needed to find out.*

FIVE

"All kids need is a little help, a little hope, and someone who believes in them"

- Magic Johnson

April 1997

As I went through the second set of entrance doors of the Oakville Hospital, the smell of the antiseptic greeted me. I was at the hospital to meet Claire, the speech and language pathologist referred to us by Dr. Pelletier.

The beige walls had peeled off, exposing minimal white paint underneath. Frenzied footsteps tread the off-white linoleum tiles in the crowded twenty-four-foot-wide lobby which most likely had its heyday fifty years ago when this hospital was built. Oakville's population had doubled since that time. Chattering and pages asking for medical help were amplified in that space. Rumors were that another hospital would be built somewhere in the area, but I had seen no construction nearby. Yet, Oakville hospital seemed to survive with the essential minimum maintenance.

The hallway was an offshoot of the lobby in its design and age. Some wheelchairs and trollies were parked on the right side as we passed by the emergency room entrance toward the Speech and Language Pathology corridor. As we turned right, we immediately found ourselves in front of the door with Claire's name and designation.

Claire seemed to be a French-Canadian too, based on her first and last name, but her accent did not give that away. With a youthful and sweet face, Clare could have been mistaken for a candidate in a beauty pageant, not a medical doctor. My guess was that she was a recent graduate in her field.

"Hello, Gordon, my name is Claire." She received us with a warm smile. *I preferred having the first appointment of the day, so we would get the attention right away.* With her statuesque frame, Claire dropped both hands on her knees as she bent down to be within Gordon's eye level. She emphasized her words, intending to capture Gordon's attention.

I held my breath for a few seconds. My thoughts circled in infinite loops in the hopes I would witness a transformation today. *Could she make Gordon respond in some way? Maybe, at least, make him nod or shake his head?*

Dressing him up this morning reminded me of my days playing with my dolls and having a one-way conversation, except that he babbled if that was any response at all. I wish I could translate those babbles. I wish I could read his thoughts.

With puckered lips, I resigned in my hope for that transformation. With me or with a professional, Gordon carried the same pleasant, contented facial expression. I wondered if he had any inclination for our visit.

"Come over here, Gordon." She held his hand and led him to a play area where they could sit on the floor. Gordon showed no resistance and walked alongside her. Then, facing me, she said, "Let me work with him while you stay right outside the room."

I stared at my empty hands then crossed my arms, having witnessed what seemed like a kidnapping situation. My son would just go with whoever would lead him.

From where I was asked to stay, I observed through the glass window. Claire held up a toy, talking and tickling Gordon, yet nothing she did triggered a response. As predicted, Gordon preferred to do what fascinated him and not what other people thought would interest him. He picked up a toy and twirled it like a baton, accompanied by his babbles and sudden laughter. Tears welled up in my eyes. *He was supposed to start school in six months. How would he cope?*

After a little while, Claire and Gordon emerged from the play area and walked toward me. Facing him, she said, "Gordon, give me a moment while I talk to your mom, okay?" Gordon looked straight ahead; like a horse with blinders, he did not seem to have any peripheral vision. She escorted Gordon to the waiting room's play area, then approached me.

"Please have a seat." Claire took the chair beside the one she indicated.

Leaning forward, Claire delivered her observations while holding on to her clipboard of notes. "I say his receptive language is at sixteen months old."

My palms moistened. "What does that mean?"

"Today, he is forty-two months; that's three and a half years old, yet his understanding is equivalent to a child at sixteen months."

"Huh?" I reacted with a breaking voice. My eyes opened wide. I was at a loss for words.

"If you notice, Gordon responds to noises but not to his name."

"You mean, he doesn't know his name?" My hand clung to my chest, my heart roaring like thunder.

She looked me in the eye. "Do you call him by his name, *Gordon*?"

"Of course, how else should I call him?"

Leaning against the chair, she continued. "Some parents address their kid as 'sweetie' or 'baby,' and that could be confusing to some children."

"I sometimes call him by those terms of endearment, but at most times, we just call him Gordon."

"I suggest that you continue calling and referring to him by his name. Let's be consistent, at least, until we sense he is responding to his name."

"Okay, I'll keep that in mind."

She glanced at her notes, then scrolled down to her next discussion item. "He also has difficulty understanding simple directions, even with gestures."

I rubbed my clammy hands together while I held my breath as I listened to Claire continue to explain the observations she made.

"And on the expressive side, he scores at an age equivalent to ten months." Her voice was devoid of emotion and as clinical as I expected.

"You mean, you expect a ten-month-old baby to talk?" *Wasn't that an exaggeration? Could he not be given an age equivalency of twelve months or eighteen months?* But then again, whatever age she gave, my son was very much behind by over two years.

"I observed vowel sounds, hums, and babbles. That's a ten-month-old stage. After that stage, a toddler around twelve months will make gestures, for example pointing." She demonstrated the gesture.

I listened intently, realizing that I also had not seen Gordon doing any pointing.

"Take a deaf-mute for example." She motioned with her hands and continued. "By the time the kid is a year old, he takes your hand, asking you to reach something for them. We say a deaf-mute has gestural communication."

I agreed with her. Gordon did not do that. Instead, he helped himself. He climbed up the cupboard to get his own glass, without a word and without asking for help. And, all the while, I thought that was a good thing, that he was being independent.

"Overall, my assessment is severe. I can't further evaluate him for articulation and phonology because of his limited ability of expressive language. I also observed fleeting eye contact."

I blanked out after she finished explaining her assessment. *What could be more severe than that?*

"Anything else?" My chest tightened, and I didn't know if I could bear more unpleasant news. "What do we do? Is there a possibility that Gordon will talk?"

I glanced at Gordon, happy and contented but absorbed in his own world. Tears were about to trickle from my eyelids, but I controlled them. He didn't seem to have a need or desire to reach out to me or any human being. *Yet, I knew in my heart Gordon was happy.*

"I have some ideas for promoting speech." She took a sheet of paper with a list of suggestions from the stack of files and handed them to me. "And I'd like to see him every six to eight weeks."

I wasn't sure if she was avoiding my question, or if she just didn't want to tell me that my son would babble all his life. or if she can't really predict the future. Did she give the same sheet of suggestions to all her clients? Suggestions which included: model counting numbers and alphabet, use finger plays, use exaggerated sing-song verbalizations to enhance a child's attention and more. *Hadn't we been doing this since birth? Maybe it was not enough.*

SIX

"Every student can learn, just not on the same day,
or in the same way."

– John Evans

June 1997

It had been five months since Gordon was diagnosed, five months since he started going to the YMCA daycare, and five months that I had held out hope that he would call me 'Mom.' Even though my head still spun with the ramifications of the diagnosis, I reminded myself that I was Patrick's mom, and he needed me too.

Rays of sunlight streamed through the window into our living room where I sat in the rocking chair and watched my two children, seven-year-old Patrick and three-year-old Gordon, immersed in their own pastimes. The soothing music of Patrick's piece from the *Bastien Piano Book* filled the air as he played the piano to prepare for his Father's Day recital.

"Good job, Patrick." I applauded warmly as he concluded. The hair at my nape prickled each time I heard my son play his piece. He swayed to the music and was not just playing his piece but emoting to the tune of the music, a mark of a promising musician.

As I analyzed his expressions, I saw features of Bingo in him, his lanky stature, bushy eyebrows, and creased forehead.

A faint rumbling sound intruded at that moment, and my gaze shifted to Gordon maneuvering his Matchbox car back and forth within six inches on the coffee table while babbling to himself, followed by giggles only he could relate to.

"Gordon! Can you please keep quiet?" Patrick raised his voice, yet Gordon ignored him. I held my breath, realizing something might ruin this peaceful afternoon.

Without giving Gordon a second chance, Patrick cleared his throat, faced me, and asked for my help in his whining tone. "Mom, can you please tell Gordon to keep quiet?"

I nodded. *I figured it must a challenge for him to focus on his piece.*

I moved closer to Gordon and cupped my hands on his chubby pumpkin cheek. I gave him a gentle squeeze while I whispered to get his attention. "Gordon, sweetie pie, pumpkin pie."

Despite my use of actions, Gordon continued to be unresponsive to my cues. He carried on with his play.

This time, I clutched his toy car and spoke in a hushed tone. "Hush. Patrick is practicing his piano lessons. We need to respect your brother."

I was not sure if he understood that, or perhaps he didn't care. He did not face me. He lowered his head instead, peering through the tabletop akin to a professional cake decorator when he would level the icing on the cake. Baffled, I wondered what he could see from that angle other than dust on the table.

Patrick grunted as he flipped his music book, getting ready to play another piece. "Mom, the sound bothers me. Why doesn't he listen to you?"

"I'm sorry, Patrick; this won't happen again." Biting my lower lip, I covered my face. *Why did I say that?*

Not wanting a stressful Sunday afternoon, I grasped Gordon's hand and carry him. "Come, let's go to Dad." He did not resist. We moved to the family room where Bingo was watching the Toronto Blue Jays baseball game on TV. Gordon continued with his ritual on the coffee table, oblivious to Bingo and me.

Bingo and I exchanged glances. He nodded, understanding that Patrick needed his space to practice for his piano recital. Heaving a sigh, I headed back to the living room and listened to Patrick practice his piano pieces. I was in awe at how much he had progressed since he'd started lessons two years ago. That also made me wonder how so much had changed in our lives during the past nine years of living in Canada—more dramatically in the last six and a half years. Barely six weeks before giving birth to Patrick in January 1990, Bingo had gotten his job at the bank. Eight months into his job, we moved out of that rented semi-detached home and into this townhome.

Everything about my two boys was as different as a zipper and a button. As a newborn, Patrick looked like an old woman with wrinkled skin. With his arched eyebrows prominent at birth, he looked like he was already thinking deeply about his presence in this new world. Newborn Gordon was wrinkle-free and chubby, with a pleasant expression. It was easy to fall in love with my media-perfect baby model.

When Patrick had not strung words together at two and a half years old, they had advised us to speak one language at home—only English. By age three, just when he learned to talk, we could not stop him.

But Gordon was now almost four years old, and his babbling had not yet progressed into words. I used to take this vocalization as an encouraging sign, but now I wondered. *Would he be able to communicate with us using words?* While inside his playpen, he stood up and delivered his orations of babble. Accompanied by his hand motions, his act reminded me of a politician trying to give an emotional plea, overdramatizing his words. Dumbfounded, I wondered if he intended to get our attention with his babbling. Or did he find babbling soothing?

The music stopped, and Patrick announced that he was done playing the piano. "Mom, what did you think of that? Did you like it?"

"Mom. Mom," he said, raising his volume a tad to get my attention.

I bolted upright and stretched my arms from the rocking chair. "Yes, Pat, you did great. Keep up the good work. You're more than ready for the recital."

With a somber tone, he asked, "Mom, what's wrong with Gordon?"

I shifted my gaze to the window, eyeing the lilac bushes which seemed to have grown faster than

I expected. I felt a sob rising in my throat. "What do you mean?"

"He doesn't want to play with me anymore. He just plays by himself and makes that weird sound all the time."

"I don't know, Pat." I faced him, wondering how to explain to him that his brother has autism. "Why don't you come over and sit with me in the couch. And, grab that blue photo album." I pointed to the albums on the bottom shelf.

"You mean Gordon's first-year photos?" His eyes glistened, and he glanced sideways.

"Yup." Patrick loved looking at photos and hearing about the background story. He joined me on the couch, sitting in a lotus position, and flipped through the album.

I held him close, so he could lean on my chest, then I asked, "What do you remember when Gordon was born?"

"I don't know. That one?" He pointed to a photo taken at the hospital.

A grin played on my lips as I recalled that fateful day. "I was expecting to give birth to your brother around Halloween. Dad and I were watching TV, excited about the Blue Jays' chance at winning the World Series for the second time. That's the baseball championship, Pat." We were a Blue Jays family then. Our team was World

Series champion last year, and here they were, vying for the back-to-back victory.

In a slow, well-paced response, he said, "I remember… playing with my Thomas trains." I'm not sure if that was his memory because we had been narrating this scene often.

"Yes, that one too. After the game, I felt a pain in my tummy. Dad and I thought I was just excited that the Toronto Blue Jays won."

"What happened after that, Mom?" He prodded, eager to know more.

I stroked his cheek. "The game ended past midnight. You were fast asleep." Like Bingo, his inquisitive facial expression included raised brows. "But Dad had to dress you up and carry you to the car."

"Did I cry?"

"Nah. He just whispered, 'Pat, wake up. The baby might come out now. We need to bring Mom to the hospital.'"

Gordon was born an hour after we reached the hospital. *Answered prayers* must have been in Patrick's thoughts as he beamed from ear to ear for his first picture with his future playmate.

"Can we name him 'Gordon'?" Patrick eagerly suggested, referring to the Gordon train in the Thomas the Tank Engine series. That name stuck. He would be like the train, Gordon who was feisty and fierce-looking but always had the heart to extend himself to others. My tough guy.

Patrick flipped to the next page and pointed to a picture where a woman was playing with Gordon.

"Pat, that's my aunt, my Tita Tita. Lolo's sister." If that picture could talk, we would hear Tita Tita cooing over Gordon. Here, Gordon had his arms outstretched while giggling in response. I examined the picture. A knot formed in my stomach shortly after. If one of autism's symptoms is unresponsiveness, this picture was hard proof he could not have been born with autism. His autism came later on in life.

"Look at Gordon. He's laughing. How old was he here?" He traced the photo with his finger.

I studied the photo. "He could have been just three months."

"Was I like that at three months?" Patrick asked.

"What do you mean?"

"Did I also laugh at three months old?"

"Pat, check these out." I showed him some of his baby pictures. "We couldn't get any reaction from you at four months old. Pat, you were already in deep thought when you were a baby."

"How old was I when I first laughed?"

I tickled him, and he burst into soft giggles. "You're laughing now."

His laughter stopped. "Seriously, Mom, when did I first laugh?"

"Maybe five or six months?"

"Mom, I remember this." He was pointing to a picture I took of Gordon seated on my friend's lap. Gordon turned his head, laughing at his brother's antics. "Why didn't I laugh like Gordon?" He looked at me, imitating Gordon's laughter.

This time, I gave Patrick a tight squeeze and kissed his forehead. "Ha-ha. You're funny, Pat. There you go. You laugh like Gordon." I paused. "Look, we're all unique in our ways, and it doesn't mean you and Gordon have to be the same at everything. You're both so different but equally lovable." I tickled his ribs once again which caused him to explode into laughter.

We browsed more pages and spotted a photo of Bingo reading a story while the two boys fixed their gazes on a book. Another picture displayed Gordon kneeling on the piano bench while he banged his fists on the piano. "Mom, Gordon always does that after I practice."

I nodded, not knowing what to say.

"How about this one, Mom? And this one? And this one?" Patrick wanted to know more stories behind each picture.

After perusing the album, Patrick's tone turned somber. "Mom. I'm bored."

"What do you mean? I don't see you playing with your brother anymore."

"He doesn't want to play with me. When I try to play with him, he just walks away."

"Maybe. Maybe, we just need to get closer to him, Pat. What do you think?" I wondered if Gordon had some hearing issues.

"It's not like that, Mom," he went on. "I mean… remember when we used to run our trains on the tracks? He refuses to play trains like that with me anymore. He'd take the train and run it on the table, just like what he did here. And…. He doesn't listen, Mom. When I say 'No,' he still keeps on playing his way."

I truly felt for Patrick. He seemed to sense my doubts, doubts I have kept from him, and doubts I could not share with him.

Tears spilled from my eyes. I looked away for a moment, hoping Patrick didn't notice, but for a seven-year-old, he seems intuitive. "Let me tell you something." Taking a deep breath, I held him tight.

With puckered lips, Patrick turned his head toward me.

"Do you remember when we went down to New Jersey one Halloween?" Patrick narrowed his eyes and lifted his chin as he tried to recall. "Remember that time when Tito Mayo and family came?"

"Yeah. I remember. All of us kids were in the family room, Gordon too."

I beamed as he recollected that timeframe. "Us adults were in the kitchen, chatting."

"What do adults talk about? I hear you talk, then laugh."

I chuckled.

"We talked about our days when we were your age where we got spend time at the beach, played out in the streets… our fond memories."

At this age, Patrick might have been too young to grasp memories, but I wanted him to know that when they reached my age, they would also reminisce about their childhood days.

"Once you get older, you'll do the same. Remember this. Gordon is the only person whom you can cherish these memories with," I said, putting much emphasis on *only*.

Patrick frowned before sprawling on the couch again. "But will Gordon ever talk? How can we talk about our childhood days, if he can't even talk?"

A knot formed in my stomach. What if Patrick was right? What if Gordon never talked? Pushing my thoughts aside, I stared outside the window at the lilacs, hoping to find answers.

Patrick nudged me, and I knew he too wanted answers.

I looked him in the eye. "I cannot promise anything, Pat, but I can only assure you about one thing. We'll do the best we can. Will you help me?"

Patrick straightened his shoulders. "What do you want me to do, Mom?"

"Be my helper, maybe?"

Patrick gave me a high five and leapt from the couch.

"Hey, hey... not too quick, Pat."

He quickly turned around.

"Come over here." With outstretched arms, I motioned for him to come closer.

"Yes, Mom."

"Let me give you a big hug. Oh, Pat, what am I going to do without you?"

He looked at me quizzically.

Gordon came running to the living room with Bingo trailing from behind. Patrick tickled Gordon, but he trailed his two Matchbox cars on the carpet and created a rumbling noise. Patrick mimicked his voice while Bingo joined me on the couch. We watched our two sons interact together, more so, how Patrick tried to get Gordon to interact with him.

A wave of tranquility washed over me. I realized that although we couldn't change Gordon's diagnosis, we could do our best together as a family.

SEVEN

*"When you judge someone based on a diagno-
sis, you miss out on their abilities, beauty, and
uniqueness."*

– Sevenly

July 1997

During the summer, we moved and settled into a single detached home. Considered a tertiary road, our road was third priority in snowplowing, which meant it remained white and icy on snowy days. A relatively short road, few non-residents drove by the area.

In the summer months, children in the neighborhood could be seen playing on the road. The homes were uniform in style, and I bet each family here, just like us, has one or two children. You could also observe a van and a car parked on the home's driveway which made you wonder what was inside the two-car garage.

New to this area, our garage still had room for our vehicles. Each lot was fifty feet wide. Every homeowner maintained his fifty-foot-deep front yard in the same manner; it made the home very inviting. Bingo and I already agreed that he would have to look after the gardening as I was not really an outdoor person nor into gardening. Not that he had a green thumb, but one of us must do it or our front yard became an eyesore in the neighborhood.

RoseAnne, our landlady at the semi-detached home where we rented a bedroom before we had children, came for a visit.

"RoseAnne, what a pleasant surprise." I lit up as soon as I saw that familiar face coming to our front door. *Who else had dirty blonde hair, was skinny, with dark-rimmed glasses and always wore a cardigan, even during the summer heat?* "Look at you; you haven't changed one bit. I missed you." I escorted her inside the house and led her to the living room where we both settled on the couch.

"It's so nice to see you, Leah. We need to catch up."

"Yes, we need to." I was nostalgic about the time we had spent together, remembering her sister who lived in downtown Toronto with a Filipino family. That family introduced me to her in 1988. She had been my landlady since then until we moved to our townhome in 1990.

"Yeah. Bingo tells me he sees you sometimes on the train."

"That's how I found out you'd moved out of that townhouse to this neighborhood. Great neighborhood! Do you like it here?" She wrinkled her nose as she studied the living room, admiring what little furniture and decorations we had. She craned her neck to check the outdoors from the inside.

"Can I offer you anything?" I motioned to stand up.

She shook her head and waved to stop me from moving on. "Don't bother. I'm good."

"We really didn't plan on moving out, but it seemed like we outgrew the townhome, plus our next-door neighbor kept complaining about the noise. After searching for a place to live, Bingo knew this was the right home for us. No long discussions and we presented our offer right away."

She chuckled. "Bingo." Her pitch rose. "That's unlike him to make such an impulsive decision, but this is a good buy. You can't go wrong with this."

"Yeah, that's what our friends say. Maybe Bingo was sick." Laughter exploded. "No regrets. I'm sure we'll be living here for a long time, considering the kids; school is just a kilometer away."

"Hey, listen, I brought these for you." She presented four seedlings inside a paper bag.

I raised my eyebrows. "What are these? What am I supposed to do with them?"

"They're plants." She knew that I knew nothing about plants. "Seedlings of boxwood plants which are great for hedges."

"They are? Where should I plant them?"

"Let's go outside so I can show you where. Somewhere in your front yard."

As we stepped outside the house, I spotted my next-door neighbor approaching the front door.

With little introduction, he blurted out, "Hey, Leah, do you know that Gordon is by himself, up the street on his tricycle." Seeing my eyeballs about to pop out, he comforted me. "But don't worry, my wife is keeping an eye on him from a distance."

"What? Oh my! Thanks for letting me know."

"Bingo," I yelled out to him.

"I'm in the backyard," he hollered back.

I raised my voice. "Gordon is up the street."

"What do you mean?" Bingo rushed into the house, gasped for breath, and joined RoseAnne and me by the front door.

"He's on his tricycle, all by himself."

We noticed that the garage door was open, and Gordon's red tricycle was missing.

Bingo's face was filled with guilt since he was known to leave the garage door ajar when he did yardwork. He darted outside while RoseAnne and I waited for him.

RoseAnne patted my back. "Don't worry, Gordon should be fine. This is a safe neighborhood."

I was tempted to share my secret about Gordon's condition, but I didn't think this was the right time. *How long would I keep this from my close friends when it was eating me inside?*

A few moments later, Bingo arrived with a firm grip on Gordon's hand while he carried the tricycle. Gordon acted as if nothing had happened.

I scooped him up in my arms, planting kisses all over his cheeks, imagining the dread of losing him. *This couldn't happen again. Ever!*

RoseAnne recognized that it was a family matter that needed to be addressed in private so she bid us goodbye and planned to catch up again soon.

Bingo proceeded to the garage and stashed the tricycle on a higher shelf.

"There." He faced Gordon. "If you want to ride your tricycle, please ask Dad, okay?"

With no reaction, Gordon darted inside the house and headed to the living room where he found his Matchbox car on the coffee table and played his favorite activity. If he could talk, he would have said, "No worries, Dad. I am happy playing with my toy car."

I watched Gordon from the hallway, wondering what went on in his brain. I wished I could read his mind.

I stared at the seedlings RoseAnne gave me earlier and handed them to Bingo.

Bingo dug a hole in the ground and shoved the boxwood seedlings in right by the walkway to the front door. On that site would sprout new ideas and thoughts in raising my family. As these boxwoods grew, they would witness our family's evolution in that home.

EIGHT

"'For I know the plans I have for you,' declares the Lord,
"plans to prosper you and not to harm you, plans you
give you hope and a future.'"

- Jeremiah 29:11

August 1997

'Back to school' advertisements filled the commercials breaks during every TV show; radio and newspaper flyers reminded us that summer break was about to conclude. Bingo and I had yet to discuss Gordon's school placement next month.

We were scheduled to meet with Mr. McMann, St. Marguerite's principal. As Bingo and I entered the school, my thoughts wandered to the first time we set foot in this building when Patrick was starting junior kindergarten. Back then, it was the school's second year of operation. On its fourth year now, the school seemed to have expanded with a lot of students requiring portable classrooms to accommodate them.

Somewhere in the corner of the school building was Mr. McMann's office, which exuded natural light. I panned the surroundings and glimpsed a family picture of him and his wife, two teenage boys, and a golden retriever mounted on a picture stand atop a gray filing cabinet. Having a teenage son, I would guess he must be in his mid-forties. Piles of papers were stacked on the credenza behind his desk.

"Good morning, Mr. and Mrs. Rivera," Mr. Mc-Mann greeted us in his low, husky voice, extending his right hand and looking up at Bingo. If Bingo was five foot ten, he must have been a few inches shorter. Canadians, we had observed in our last nine years there, were not as tall as their American counterparts. With school not yet in session, he sported a casual attire of jeans and a golf shirt that suited his build.

"Good morning," we responded, almost simultaneously.

"Have a seat. I take it that your son, Gordon, will attend St. Marguerite this school year, eh?" We settled on our seats.

"Yes, his brother, Patrick, goes to this school too."

"Patrick, I know Patrick Rivera. He was in Mrs. Dean's class last year."

I wondered if he knew all five hundred students in the school by name.

"So, what's the problem... er, special with Gordon?" he asked while brushing his salt-and-pepper beard.

"He is still non-verbal and not toilet-trained," I said matter-of-factly, wondering how many diaper changes Gordon needed in a day and if that would change when he started school.

With open hands, he leaned forward, looked at Bingo, then faced me and said, "Mr. and Mrs. Rivera, we have an inclusion policy. All our children, with a disability or not, are in the same program as other students." He paused, then carried on with emphasis. "That means, we do not segregate children with disabilities. If the child with a disability cannot cope, our school board provides an EA, an educational assistant. The EA helps the child with the tasks at hand and is also there for the child's safety."

We nodded. *Were there other families like us?*

He continued. "Our kindergarten classrooms have their own private washrooms, so children don't have to walk down the hallway."

"That's good to know, Mr. McMann. When should we inform you about our decision if he will attend this school?" Bingo felt at ease with what we just heard.

He shrugged. "Whenever you're ready."

St. Marguerite Elementary School was part of the separate school board system, which in Ontario is a Catholic public school. It was still publicly funded, and for as long as the child was Catholic and belonged to the school zone, they could not refuse the child to attend their school.

"Bingo, I am not sure I'm ready to send Gordon to school yet." I faced Bingo, speaking in our native tongue.

Bingo pursed his lips. "Mr. McMann, thank you for your time." Bingo shook his hand. "My wife and I will think about it, and we will get back to you right away."

He escorted us outside his office. "No problem. Let me know when you're ready."

Bingo didn't say a word as we passed through the hallway. I trailed behind him, scrutinizing the classrooms, wondering if Gordon would fit in. I was sure every mother of an autistic child would want them to experience some normalcy. Fear crawled down my spine. *Was that school for Gordon?*

As soon as we slid inside the Dodge Caravan, Bingo interrogated me. "Why did you chicken out? He will have an EA, anyway."

"It's not that I *chickened out*." An image of Gordon playing his repetitive activity in a corner flashed through my mind. "Don't you think he'll be the laughingstock?"

"But he has to start school sometime." He started the ignition and swerved to the right.

Bingo was right, but I refused to acknowledge that.

"We can't protect him all his life. He needs to learn to survive in this tough world."

"That's easy for you to say." Bingo loved to talk about how he learned to survive the tough way. He saw me as the lenient parent, easy to give in to a kid's whine. *Maybe he thought by forcing Gordon, he'd snap out of autism and be normal like everyone else.*

"If he skips junior kindergarten, do you think he'll be ready for senior kindergarten next year?" He raised his voice and stepped on the gas.

"I don't know," came my feeble reply. "He has to make it then… I think."

Silence crossed between us upon reaching home. He headed over to the family room to watch his sports on TV. I didn't have the heart to break the silence. I walked upstairs to my room and plopped on the edge of my bed. I couldn't understand what was happening to my son. Did anyone know? I was lost. Tears trickled down my cheeks. I couldn't deny that Gordon's condition had put a strain in my relationship with Bingo. If we talked about it, we ended up fighting. However, not talking about it wouldn't erase the fact that Gordon had autism.

***

Since our visit with Claire, the speech and language pathologist with the Oakville Trafalgar Hospital, I'd been working a lot with Gordon. When able, Patrick would assist me.

Posted on Gordon's bedroom wall were the alphabet letters.

Both kids were seated in the family room while Bingo read the sports section of the newspaper. Strapped in his high chair, which we brought in from the breakfast nook, Gordon babbled.

I attempted to attend to his needs today. "Gordon, say *A*."

"Mom, let me try." Patrick was always enthusiastic to try his ideas.

"Gordon." Patrick called on Gordon using a high-pitched voice. "Look, Gordon."

Patrick got the letter A card and brought it closer to Gordon's face. The babbles got louder, and he looked away. Patrick persisted, but Gordon shook his head from left to right like a shaken rag doll.

"Gordon, stop!" I pressed his temples while my fingers ran from the back of his head to the base of his neck. Chills ran down my spine, thinking his vertebra that connected the head and neck might snap.

"Pat, you're doing a wonderful job, but I feel we need to stop this."

Patrick lifted his chin to face me.

"Let's not force him. Not this time," I suggested.

I was out of ideas on how to teach Gordon to talk. Our method didn't seem to impact Gordon's developmental skills. He still didn't respond to us. *There had to be another way. Soon, Patrick would no longer have the patience in playing with him.*

Bingo eyed us but said nothing. He was out of ideas, I could tell. Bingo believed engaging with Gordon in some kind of play could trigger some response from Gordon. He had been bringing the boys out to the park, or they went tobogganing, but maybe incorporating some boisterous cheer would do the trick.

In the meantime, every now and then, Gordon just broke out in a rage. We had stopped giving him the milk, thinking that had triggered the outbursts. Was there something else that triggered the outbursts? At other times, for some unknown reason, he just tossed a plate or a glass. He also pulled the tablecloth, toppled down a table, or threw the TV's remote control. Most of the time, those tantrums happened when we least expected them to occur. When the tantrum subsided, and his energy was zapped, Gordon appeared to be remorseful. He looked at the broken pieces without a word. *He was an angel.*

NINE

~

"Autism is like a rainbow. It has a bright side and a darker side. But every shade is important and beautiful."

– Rosie Tennant Doran: Fellow Autist

October 1997

While Patrick dressed up for school right away, Gordon needed to be pacified before taking him to the daycare. Each time I dropped Gordon off in the mornings, butterflies fluttered in my belly as I created a mental tally of what could go wrong when he was in their care, especially when he threw one of those tantrums.

Gordon had been going to that daycare for almost ten months now, yet he still had not learned to communicate nor interact with other children. Although the reports we received from the daycare assistant sounded positive—"Gordon is happy today," "Gordon played with the sand today," "It's a beautiful day for Gordon,"—something was unsettling. I was not sure what kind of report I wanted to hear. It was evident he was happy when left on his own, doing his kind of activity.

My thoughts froze while staring at the photos the daycare sent: photos of him seated on the daycare assistant's lap by the swing and the other one where she was carrying him. *Carried at four years old?* Yes, they were cute pictures of my son, but like me, it seemed those assistants confirmed that his inability to interact and communicate *was a concern. Yet, they gave me positive reports.* I cringed.

As I arrived to pick up Gordon, I heard the upbeat music from Spice Girls' song "Stop." A smile spread across my face as I witnessed the children dancing to the rhythm with their hand actions. *Would Gordon someday dance or at least move to some rhythm?*

My smile was short-lived when I noticed that Gordon was not in the room where I usually picked him up.

"Excuse me." I approached the daycare manager. "Where's Gordon?"

"Oh, he's in the play yard with Leila," she said, referring to Gordon's daycare assistant who just completed a two-year course of Early Childhood Education from Sheridan College in Oakville. Young and enthusiastic, Leila seemed happy she got a job right away.

"Thanks."

As I approached the fenced-in play yard, I spotted Leila's blond hair and Gordon's dangling feet; he must be on Leila's lap *again*. I shook my head in disbelief. *Why did they have to carry him? Baby him?*

"Gordon, woohoo, Mom's here." I was hoping Gordon would run toward me.

Leila turned around while clinging to Gordon. "Look, Mom's here."

As soon as Gordon faced me, my body froze, and purse dropped. With eyes open wide, I couldn't believe what I was seeing. *My baby! Bruises on his face, down to his arms and to his shin.* Despite the situation, Gordon had blank stares.

"Gordon, come to Mama." Leila led him toward me.

I knelt to his level. "Gordon, are you okay?" No response from him. His gaze was somewhere else. Facing Leila, I raised my voice. "What happened here?"

"I helped him up the slide," Leila fumbled as she explained the incident. "Just when he got to the top, another boy came behind him. I went inside to get something. When I got back, I found him on the pavement."

"What?" *The pavement? The bottom of the slide was covered with rough asphalt. Why did she leave him alone?*

"You left him alone by himself?" I was not sure I heard that right.

"Er… Mrs. Rivera," her voice quivered. "Not inside. I was just by that door," she said, pointing to the entrance from the play yard to the daycare. "The daycare manager called me, and I was eyeing Gordon from a distance. Everything happened so quick, and the next thing I knew, Gordon was on the ground. I'm so sorry and hope you understand that it was an accident."

I refused to hear any more, and instead I ask, "Where's the boy?" I was eager to see what he looked like, knowing bullies should be reprimanded.

"His mom has picked him up. He's gone for the day."

I heaved a sigh. "Do the parents know what the boy did?"

"I was here with Gordon. Let me ask the manager if she has informed the parents."

Tiny prickles pinched my head, and I bit my lip, refraining from screaming. "Did you ask the boy what happened?"

"He said that he asked Gordon to come down the slide, but he wouldn't."

I rolled my eyeballs. Suddenly, I ran out of words to say. Who was to blame here? The boy or Leila for leaving them alone? *They were both at fault.*

"Leila, I need an incident report on this. I have to inform Halton Support Services and the daycare management about what happened. I expect that tomorrow when I bring Gordon in the morning."

"Yes, Mrs. Rivera."

Not wanting to deal with this situation, I grabbed Gordon's bag and motioned him to come with me. As we walked to the parking lot, I could still hear the Spice Girls tune.

Stop right now, thank you very much
I need somebody with a human touch

Yes, that's what I need right now.

***

My mind was reeling as I was holding Gordon with one hand while carrying his backpack with my other hand walking toward my nine-year-old Dodge Colt hatchback car. I was hashing out ideas on how to help Gordon, get him to talk to us, interact with us, let us know his thoughts and be with us as a family. *Why was that so hard?*

Images of the street children in the Philippines flashed in my mind. How did they learn to talk and play? Was that the new thing? *Did everyone need to see a therapist?*

I opened the door, dropped the bag, and moved the front seat forward to strap Gordon in his booster seat in the rear.

As I positioned myself in the driver's side, I noticed a familiar face seated in the car parked next to mine.

Was that Shelley, the behavior therapist Dr. Pelletier referred us to. "Shelley?" I called out to her and stepped out of the car.

"Hi, Mrs. Rivera." She waved, and I wondered why she was here.

Shelley had seen Gordon three times earlier this year. In those visits, she informed us of Gordon's limited preference for a variety of toys, mostly cars. "He is stuck with solitary play," she mentioned in our first visit. "You should encourage interactive play with him." She seemed to speak like an authority of behavior therapy.

But the biggest question was how? *How did we encourage interactive play?* She suggested more playtime while we squatted on the floor. *How did more playtime change or improve his behavior or at least get him to communicate with us?*

We had done everything the professionals had suggested. But, maybe, there was something we weren't doing right. Here we were after several visits to those therapists and doing our homework, yet Gordon's receptive skills had to still be comparable to that of a sixteen-month-old child. He had not grasped that when you went up the slide, the next thing to do was go down. He still couldn't understand that little boy's request to slide down. And he still had not learned to say *No* to mean he wouldn't slide down.

"Do you have a minute?"

With my car's tinted windows, she probably did not know that Gordon was already inside.

"Sure, what is it?"

I approached her and blurted out, "Will my son ever learn to talk?" *There was no better way to put it, but was that the reality we wished to have?*

"To be honest, Mrs. Rivera, you need to brace yourself for the future. Either he will be mute or if he gets to speak," Shelley paused as if she was finding the right words, "it will be in such a robotic manner."

I nodded. "Thank you, Shelley. Have a good day." I retreated to my car. I didn't know what I was thanking her for. Maybe her honesty? Her time?

For some professionals, working with my son was just a nine-to-five job. Whether my son responded positively to their approach, or he did not, they still got paid anyway. What did they care? My son's future was at their mercy. But I couldn't accept the fact that Gordon didn't talk, and I wouldn't give up. *I couldn't.*

Holding on to the steering wheel, I bowed my head and took a deep breath. Would there ever be hope? I looked above and gazed at the vibrant colors of the falling leaves. My tears weren't just welling up now, but like the leaves, they cascaded down my cheeks. That time, I let them flow. *My God, give me strength, give me guidance, give me wisdom.*

TEN

"If a child can't learn the way we teach, maybe we should teach the way they learn."

- Ignacio Estrada

January 1998

Five months ago, we decided not to send Gordon to school yet.

It was a new year, and we were back at Dr. Pelletier's office, a year after we consulted with him. His office was still the same since the last time we visited. As we scanned the other patients seated at the waiting reception, Bingo leaned on me and whispered, "I bet you that child also has autism."

I nudged his ribs. With my forefinger on my lips, my eyes widened, and turned to him.

"Just because you have a child with autism doesn't mean that you can assess others the same way." I talked to him in a hushed tone. Although I meant that as a tease, there was some truth in there.

I glanced at Gordon who was in the play area with the other kids, but his focus was on the building blocks. Not to build, but to run the block on the carpet back and forth in a straight line within six inches as he did with his Matchbox car. Guilt surged inside for feeling the same way. When I saw others misbehaving, I thought they may have a disability like my son.

Averting my gaze to Bingo, I asked him, "Have you seen any change in Gordon since the last time we were here?"

"Change? Yeah. He not only prefers toy cars, but he likes real cars too." He was trying to be funny in that tone, but it was true that Gordon's fascination for cars had extended to real cars. We needed to tether Gordon to be in close range with us since his eyes could scan the parking lot while his feet moved forward toward the building.

One instance was at a Walmart parking lot wherein as soon as we got out of the store, Gordon walked over to a van, scanned the exterior, and tiptoed to check the interior, especially the dashboard, acting like a potential buyer or someone with some ill intent.

Afraid that his van would be carjacked or vandalized, the owner approached Gordon and said, "Excuse me, may I help you?"

Bingo inched his way and whispered, "Ahem, my son has autism. He happens to love vans. Don't you worry, I'm right here behind him and will pull him in a second."

This had happened several times. Some owners were accommodating and, in fact, opened their doors to allow Gordon a full view of the interior and savored his fascination. Some owners gave us that *get out of here* look. Concerned for his safety, we applied for a handicap license plate to allow us to park nearer to the building. The application required Dr. Bell's signature to certify his diagnosis. Dr. Bell asked why a child with autism needed a handicap license plate during our last visit and was reluctant to sign the form.

Just when Bingo explained his fascination for cars, Gordon rose from his seat and leaned forward on the windowsill to get a view of the cars below from Dr. Bell's third-floor clinic.

I pressed Bingo for his past year's recollections. "Seriously, I mean… in a positive way."

Bingo shrugged. "I'd like to say we're moving forward, but it's like three steps forward, two steps back."

"What do you mean?"

"Do you remember the group photo during the family reunion? He didn't want to face the camera, so his face had to be Photoshopped. And to think, when he was younger, he loved to pose in front of the camera. We need to master how to cut-and-paste pictures then."

"True, that's sad." Mist filled my eyes.

"Do you also recall when the daycare said that they don't want Gordon to take part in their Christmas program because he will ruin it for other children and the other parents will not like that."

I heaved a sigh. "If Gordon doesn't change, what memories will we have?"

"Don't jump to conclusions right away. Let's see what the doctor says."

"I hope the doctor sees some progress we may have not noticed, or maybe he has other suggestions for us."

I puckered my lips and zipped my mouth. Bingo hated it when I speculated. I crossed my legs. "Hmm, that's what we're here for."

My thoughts wandered to the books I'd read this past year. One book was about an autistic child who outgrew his behavior toward the latter part of his childhood and graduated from university. *Really? Would Gordon just snap out of it?*

I glanced at Gordon again, hoping to see any changes in his activity, but he was still fixated with the blocks and hadn't changed position.

Bingo tapped my forearm. "C'mon, Leah. Let's go, it's our turn."

I rose, hoping the doctor could ease my nerves.

Bingo approached Gordon and followed me inside Dr. Pelletier's office.

Bingo and I sat opposite one another and across from Dr. Pelletier. I propped Gordon up to sit in the empty chair beside me. Dr. Pelletier leaned closer to Gordon then knelt down to be within Gordon's eye level.

"Hello, Gordon," Dr. Pelletier said. "Do you remember me?"

Bingo and I observed them. I hoped that Gordon caught our eye signal giving him the cue. "Go ahead, say hi to that man."

Instead, Gordon kept staring above at the ceiling and broke into laughter. A few moments later, Gordon twirled his wrist like he was holding a ball and babbled. Dr. Pelletier tickled Gordon. The latter made him jerk, but he carried on with his repetitive activity. Nothing that Dr. Pelletier did interest him. Nothing got his attention. He didn't get annoyed nor fascinated with the doctor's antics.

Dr. Pelletier rose from the floor and headed back to his desk. His lips formed a thin line. "This isn't rocket science. Your son is autistic."

Bingo and I exchanged glances. If the diagnosis Dr. Pelletier made twelve months ago felt as if we were being run over by a truck, this time it was a tsunami that just walloped us with the truck included. He had just banged the gavel and delivered his verdict. There was no escaping it now.

Anger was churning within me. Stunned, I managed to maintain my silence for fear I would say things I didn't mean to.

"Is there anything else we can do?" Bingo asked with arched eyebrows.

"Just continue doing what you're doing." Dr. Pelletier didn't bother to look us in the eye as he escorted us to the door.

His lack of compassion baffled us. Was it normal for a psychiatrist to belittle his patients? He made us feel that our visit was a waste of his time. In as much as I felt crushed, I didn't feel a tear welling up anymore. My tears had dried up. I could feel my heart beat as heat flushed through my body.

Just like his office that seemed misplaced in his hospital with a welcoming atrium, he could not be a real doctor with a passion and interest in his patients' well-being.

Bingo and I didn't say a word as we crossed the hallway, down the atrium, and headed to the parking lot. Gordon babbled away, and I often wondered if he would snap out of it.

As soon as we stepped inside the car, Bingo blurted out, "What an idiot that doctor is!"

"Welcome to this world, Bingo," I acknowledged with some sarcasm. "In this world we live in, our health is at the mercy of the public purse. What does he care? Is anyone keeping a score on how they're doing?"

He stepped on the gas and swerved to the right. "Perhaps you should report him to the Ontario College of Physicians and Surgeons. How dare he talk to us like that?"

"Yup, I have to do that," I said with much determination. "His attitude toward patients cannot be tolerated." I was positive that there were complaints about this doctor, but it still didn't change the fact that Gordon had autism.

ELEVEN

"There needs to be a lot more emphasis on what a child CAN DO instead of what he can not do."

– Dr. Temple Grandin

March 1998

For the last two months, since our visit with Dr. Pelletier, his words floated in my mind and continued to shake me up and keep me awake at night as I tried to envision Gordon's adult life.

Saturday breakfast in our home was always at eight in the morning. Bingo detested the idea in the beginning, but he had since realized that sometimes a wife got the last say. Raised by a mother who did not believe in sleeping in on the weekends, I believed in passing that tradition to my family. Since we always rushed during the weekdays, Saturday mornings were the only time we could have a relaxing breakfast and a pleasant conversation.

Patrick came rushing down the stairs and reached out to kiss me. "Good morning, Mom."

"Good morning, Pat. Don't you just love seeing the snow lining on the leafless branches?" I drew his attention to the view of the lilac tree outside, but he didn't appreciate beauty from my perspective. The contrasting view of the leafless branches outside beside the kitchen's floral wallpaper was such a lovely sight. If it were up to the calendar, spring would come next week, yet it seemed winter was extending its stay with us.

Patrick, who was now eight and a half years old, helped me set the table as he salivated for the bacon. Its aroma was empowering.

Bingo declared their presence as he and Gordon scurried into the kitchen, Bingo holding Gordon's hand.

We all settled into the same seats as we always did. It was not a house rule to have a permanent seating arrangement but more a habit. Gordon was now seated in an *adult chair* like the rest of us at the breakfast nook. We stored his high chair in the basement. Although Gordon did not behave like a four-year-old child, I liked to treat him like a child his age.

"Gordon, say aahh." I cut a piece of bacon, eggs, and rice.

Gordon stared outside the window.

All of us took turns getting Gordon's attention, much like adults did when they fussed over a newborn baby. Yet, he did not manifest any interest in us nor in any activity. He continued to play with the spoon or any object and babbled during mealtime. In between feeding, he laughed for no apparent reason from our perspective.

The phone rang. Bingo grabbed the phone latched on the wall across the sink peninsula that divided the kitchen area and the breakfast nook. It was Bingo's high school classmate, Ryan, who had settled in Michigan where he now practiced medicine in pediatrics.

After a quick chat, he covered the mouthpiece, eyed at me and spoke in a hushed tone. "Do you want to talk to Ryan?"

He had always thought I had a better grasp on the medical area.

"Okay, can you feed Gordon?"

Bingo nodded to acknowledge that he would take over the feeding.

"Hey, Ryan, how's everything?"

"Not bad. Can't complain." He gave me a rundown on everyone in the family, his wife, and three boys.

"Listen." I proceeded to take the opportunity of obtaining some medical advice. "Do you think my Gordon has autism?" The subject always kept me awake.

"I can't tell. It's been more than a year since the last time I saw Gordon."

"What do you know about autism?" I pressed the issue.

"A bit. Why don't we check DSM-IV," he suggested, referring to the Diagnostic and Statistic Manual for Mental Disorders.

"Hold on, let me get a pen and a paper." Holding the pen with my right hand, I rested my elbow on the counter.

"How old did you say Gordon is?"

"Four years and five months."

"There are only three criteria," he said.

"First, it is the social aspect. Does he make friends? Or ask you to do something for him? Second, it is language."

"No. He avoids us. He stays away. All he does is just babble. No coherent words." I jotted down notes while glancing at my family. "And the third is?" I closed my eyes to visualize Gordon's daily behavior. As I relayed those behaviors to him, my mind raced and assumed the worst-case scenario.

"Not even *No*?"

"That's right. If he likes nothing, he throws it away. So, what's the third?" I felt elephants roaring in my stomach.

"Any repetitive behavior or interests?"

"Lots. He can run his car back and forth within six inches for a whole day. He twirls or spins an object. He is fascinated and keeps staring at the ceiling fan when it's turned on." I felt my throat constrict every time I shared more information.

Without asking the final question, we both acknowledged that Gordon's behavior fit the classic definition of autism. I thanked Ryan for his guidance and closed my eyes.

While I was grateful for that edification, I was also angry at Dr. Pelletier. He had no patience in explaining to us what classic autism was about. He dismissed us right away. He had no empathy for his patients.

I headed back to the breakfast nook but couldn't seem to find the appetite to finish my food. Bingo and I discussed what Ryan and I spoke about. He listened while I tried to put on a cheery smile for the family, but my head was spinning as I planned my next steps.

Once breakfast was over, I rubbed Bingo's shoulders. His shoulders dropped, and his expressionless eyes stared at nothing.

One thing for sure, we were on the same page. We were convinced that our son had autism. Unlike a developmental delay, he needed BIG HELP.

TWELVE

"As special needs parents we don't have the power to make life "fair," but we do have the power to make life joyful."

– Anonymous

May 1998

Every year, the significance of Mother's Day has changed for me. What the New Year, in its promise of new beginnings, had not fulfilled to this day, I wrapped myself with hope for that day when Gordon would call me 'Mom.'

Fine dining could have been my choice for my Mother's Day treat. Today, we choose the Swiss Chalet Restaurant not only because of its proximity from home but more so, because it is family friendly. In case Gordon made a mess, in our experience, they were accommodating and considerate. Other than that, I knew he hated waiting. Especially when we were in public, surrounded by stimuli, I could no longer predict his behavior. He just shoved a plate or a glass for whatever reason. I could only surmise that it was his non-verbal way of saying, *I don't like*. Here we were, lunching at two in the afternoon, the least busy time of their Sunday.

While waiting for our order to be served, Patrick cracked a joke that triggered us to laugh. If someone could snap an image of us giggling and enjoying each other's company right then during our late lunch at Swiss Chalet, the photo would depict us as one happy family because we were. But if that same image included audio which focused on Gordon, it would raise a flag and concern for a boy who seemed to be oblivious to his surroundings. My son, at four and a half years old, sat in a high chair, was being fed, babbled to himself, and twirled objects which prompted a stranger to take a second look at us; he was a striking contrast to the boy at the next table who seemed to be Gordon's age and could have been his classmate in junior kindergarten.

I ignored him, pushing my thoughts aside, and reminded myself that today was Mother's Day. My family was well and healthy. After lunch was over, we stepped outside with full stomachs and grateful hearts. Tethering Gordon, Bingo led the way during our stroll toward the house. With Bingo at the helm, he and Gordon marched as if they were competing for a walkathon, determined to get to their destination without delay, Bingo not giving Gordon a chance to wander. Patrick and I trailed behind and took our time. It was just a five-hundred-meter walk, anyway; we could not be very much behind. We chatted as we admired the beauty this spring day brought. White magnolias, lavender lilacs, and even the yellow dandelions were in bloom.

"They're back," Patrick drew my attention to the flying geese above in their V-formation.

Flowers in bloom, the return of the geese who migrated south during the winter, and the warmth of the spring day sun were testaments of a new beginning and a restart of our journey ahead. How forgiving life had been. I was grateful.

Snapping out of my reverie, I sung a variation of a tune inside me, as I whispered, "My God, make me a mom the second time, please." I had two boys but only one called me Mom. *Did Gordon know I was his mom?*

***

Spending Mother's Day yesterday was a sweet reprieve because the nagging frustration with Gordon's doctors and other professionals continued to haunt me. I had decided to take matters into my own hands. I clung to the steering wheel and eyed the distinct and charming homes within the boundary of Oakville. As I maneuvered to the left, my thoughts wandered over the email conversation I had with my friend and co-worker, Elma, which compelled me to visit this neighborhood.

Elma included me in the group email conversation with our former office mates. We were catching up on how our lives had been, and I had informed her I had an eight-year-old and four-and-a-half-year-old who was still not verbal and not potty-trained.

My introduction caught Elma's curiosity. In a private email, in what seemed to be worded with caution, she asked, "Do you think your younger boy has autism?"

"That's what we were told," I replied with some reservation. Bingo and I were satisfied with Ryan's confirmation of Gordon's diagnosis. Since he was still not verbal despite the therapies and his exposure to other children at the daycare, we continued to have difficulty applying the word 'autism' to refer to our family.

"Have you heard of ABA, Applied Behavior Analysis and Dr. Lovaas?" Elma asked me with curiosity.

I had been checking the library for autism-related books but never came across that term, which now piqued my interest. At that point, I was willing to attempt any new approach since the strategies used by professionals we'd worked with in the last eighteen months had not made a dent in my son's developmental progress.

With the internet as my guide, and the new search key to use in my research, my hopes soared. How fortunate that I was finding substantial information on the subject. I felt like a whole new world of strategies had been presented to me.

I recalled the evening when I approached Bingo in the family room where he was reading the newspaper while Patrick was watching *The Lawrence Welk* show on TV, and Gordon was running his cars back and forth on the coffee table. We may not have agreed on a few things, but we found time to air our thoughts. In the end, I always listened to my instinct. *A mother knows when something is wrong.*

After several evenings of internet readings, I gathered information to share with my husband. "Listen to this, ABA is a therapy used to increase the good behavior using positive reinforcements."

"What do you mean, positive reinforcements?" he asked without setting the newspaper aside.

"Just like in Marineland when they give the sea lions treats after a good performance. In doing so, those animals will come to realize that they have to follow orders to obtain treats."

"What are you insinuating? Give our son some treats? Like what?" He turned his head slightly toward me with an arched right eyebrow. "Perhaps chips or cookies that will force him to respond. My friend Elma informed me about Dr. Lovaas who tried this experiment at UCLA. She believes that when conducted with intensity and the power of the reinforcements, you will witness positive changes in their behavior."

"That sounds quite simplistic. There's got to be more to that." He went back to reading his newspaper.

"It's true and is effective," I replied in an excited tone. "Dr. Lovaas helps to popularize this approach and performed his own experiment where those who were subjected to a one-on-one therapy over forty hours per week made significant developmental gains within a few months."

"If his approach is effective, Shelley, Gordon's behavior therapist, should have mentioned this to us." Bingo was always wary of quick scams.

I gestured with open palms. "We would think so, yet I don't know why she didn't inform us about this approach."

Regardless of his indifference, I was still pumped up with this new discovery and kept searching the internet for answers. There was no way I would give up on Gordon.

Lo and behold. It must have been a godsend when I found a name and a contact number on the internet of a family who had been using this ABA. To top it all off, a woman, her name was Sandra, lived in my city which led me to call her, and we agreed to meet today.

I pulled into the asphalt driveway and strode to the red front door then rang the doorbell. *This was it.*

"Hi, Leah. Come in," Sandra, whose voice I recognized from our phone conversation, opened the door while wearing a pair of sweatpants and a long-sleeved shirt. She led me inside her home.

"Hi, Sandra." I stepped inside the foyer and removed my running shoes. Taking off shoes before entering someone's house seemed to be a Canadian custom which I had to get used to since I migrated ten years ago. After exchanging a few pleasantries, we got to the purpose of my visit.

"We've been following ABA for close to two years now," she said as she headed over to the living room while I trailed behind. She had converted the area into an ABA room. Her interior reminded me of a quaint, rustic cottage, with the natural wood color dominating the motif but now was accented with the shades of a play area.

"We conduct the program in this area." Sandra gestured to the child-size table and two chairs in one corner. I surveyed the area and spotted a kitchen set in one corner, a huge dollhouse, a bin of small toys in another corner, and more bins for little items. Everything had a label, just like a daycare environment.

We moved over to the dining room where I waited for Sandra to prepare chamomile tea.

Moments later, she appeared with two cups of tea and cookies.

"When you said, 'you've been following,' what do you mean? How is this therapy done?" I was curious. "Is someone helping you? How do you know what to teach?" Millions of questions crowded my thoughts. With the tendency to talk fast when excited, I reminded myself to spit my thoughts out one at a time.

"Oh, yes." She smiled, acknowledging my excitement. "Have you heard of Autism Services?"

"Never heard of it." I shrugged my shoulders.

"They are a service provider that provides excellent help." She took a sip of her tea. "I came across them when I needed help for my autistic daughter. Autism Services oversees my daughter's program. Before we started, they came to my home to assess my daughter's developmental needs and strengths and based on their assessment, they designed a curriculum for her special needs."

"That's amazing." My mind was now reeling with how they could do this for Gordon.

"I hired four workers, which they trained what to teach and how to teach."

I panned the room, and visuals of a one-on-one child-to-worker program came to mind. Stirring my tea, I asked, "Are they located here in Toronto?"

"They're based in California, but they have a satellite office here in downtown Toronto. You need not take a trip to Toronto. Everything happens here in my home." She paused, rose from her seat, and headed to get a notebook of numbers placed on the top of the corner table near the wall telephone. She flipped to a page and returned to the dining area to show me the number.

I noted the number on my Palm Pilot. "How's your daughter now? I mean, compared to her peers."

"Her last assessment showed that she's almost at par. She's in school now, by the way."

"Really?" With eyes open wide, my jaw dropped. *If her daughter could attend school with the other kids with no disabilities, then so could Gordon.* "How do I get started?"

"Call Autism Services. They're very helpful. At the same time, get ahold of these." She reached out for a couple of books lying on top of the other end of the dining table. I wanted to borrow hers so I could start reading right away but hesitated to ask. "I don't think they're available just anywhere, but there's a store in downtown Toronto, Parent Bookstore, that carries them."

I made a mental note of the info she provided.

Up until that time, professionals had given me some *pep* talk on what autism is all about while I trod in the murky *autism* waters. *Just keep treading, you're doing great,* they consoled me from above the ground. Today, someone had tossed me the glimmer-of-hope rope to get me out of this twenty-foot-deep well. *Help was on the way, but the help comes with you helping yourself.*

I felt my heart palpitate, and my head raced with questions to ask as our conversation fired back and forth rapidly. *Slow down*, I said to myself for fear I would miss some key information. I'd always thought that all individuals with autism would end up in the institution much like Raymond in the movie *Rain Man*, but for the first time, I saw the hope that my son would be with us till death did we part.

"One more thing." I took a sip of the tea, holding the mug with both hands, sensing the warmth of the beverage that calmed me.

She nodded, her demeanor spelling patience, and I was now more enlightened that there were options for Gordon.

"Are there other families using this ABA?"

"Hmm. There must be three of us families here in Oakville. I don't know about other areas."

"Huh?" For the first time, I realized how isolated I had been. *There were other families with autism in my town?* I had been alone in my well when my son needed help, and help was just within our midst.

"Hey." She glanced at the clock. "I'm sorry to cut you off, but I need to pick up my daughter."

"No problem. You've given me so much information today. Thank you so, so much." I rose from my seat.

"You're welcome." She shook my hand. "It's been a pleasure."

As I marched down the path, I turned around. "Sandra, Happy Mother's Day." Catching a glimpse of the lilac blooms in her front yard reminded me that a special day was set aside for us mothers to celebrate the many hats we wore, and most of all for providing unconditional love to our children.

She inched closer to me, and we parted after a tight embrace. I closed my eyes, tears welling up. We shared a moment of silence, then she bid me farewell. *Thank you, Sandra, for having given me a glimmer of hope.*

THIRTEEN

"Never discourage anyone who continually makes progress, no matter how slow."

– Plato

July 1998

While Bingo and the boys were at home, I waited at the arrival area of the Toronto Pearson International Airport to meet Rose.

Two years ago, my cousin introduced us to her friend Rose, who had asked through email about coming to Canada as a nanny under the Live-In Caregiver Program. I had never thought of hiring a nanny back then, considering Gordon would be school ready by the time her visa would have gotten approved, but that wasn't the case.

Thank goodness, we were having a reprieve from the recent heat wave. Coming from the Philippines where humidity existed, Toronto welcomed Rose in the cool and cozy weather. I also hailed the ray of hope she brought which would help me launch the ABA program. I'd looked forward to her arrival for three weeks, ever since I'd learned her visa got approved. *Help, just when I needed it most, was here.*

Saturday evening around six o'clock seemed to be a popular arrival time for flights from Asia and the Middle East. I scanned the arrival area swarmed with excited greeters, and I squeezed myself to the front of the crowd to grab that perfect spot visible to the incoming passengers. I caught myself forcing a smile and nodding as I waited for Rose's arrival. I held a Bristol board with Rose's name written on it as I waited for her arrival.

As part of the Live-In Caregiver Program requirements, Rose was interviewed in the Canadian embassy in Manila on her skill to perform household tasks. Without a doubt, she must have impressed the visa officer. I puckered my lips and narrowed my eyes as a knot formed inside my stomach. I had to inform Rose that besides her household tasks, she would be my partner in Gordon's home program.

Autism Services, the service provider who managed Sandra's home program, could not accommodate me. Staffed with two personnel in their Toronto satellite office, their waiting list was about nine months. I couldn't wait. Rose's arrival could not have come at a more perfect time. I hoped Rose fit into my plan. I thanked the heavens for sending her my way.

While waiting for Rose to appear, thoughts about Gordon's ABA program unfurled in my mind, taking me back to the past two months I had been working one-on-one sessions with him with the tips provided by Sandra during that lone visit, readings from the recommended books Bingo got for me, and other leads on the internet.

Unlike Bingo who worked in downtown Toronto and relied on the train schedule, I had more flexibility with my working hours since I took my car to and from work. My routine after work involved picking up Patrick from the sitter's place and Gordon at the daycare, and by five thirty in the afternoon, we were home. Bingo arrived home around six o'clock. While Patrick headed straight to the family room to watch TV, Gordon and I got to work together.

As soon as we got home, like someone on a mission, I headed straight to my room to change into comfortable attire, shorts, and a T-shirt on this summer day.

My palms had sweat knowing that was my first day, and I couldn't expect much. "Come, Gordon, let's go to work." I held his left hand while his right hand grasped the Matchbox car. My other hand carried a small bowl of chips. We proceeded upstairs to the guest room where we did our sessions.

Taking each step, I counted out loud, "One, two, three." He may not have imitated me then, but I had hoped someday he would.

Settling into the guest room, I propped Gordon on the high chair, fastened his belt, and secured it with its table tray. Gordon continued to cling to his Matchbox car. My reinforcements of chips were displayed in his full view.

"Gordon." I delivered my command.

Bang, bang, bang. He tapped on the high chair tray and looked above.

I repeated my command but received the same reaction from him. *He did not look at me.*

We were working on attention skills. I expected him to stop what he was doing and look at me when I called his name, but it was not working. The sight of the reinforcement was supposed to be powerful enough to entice him to comply with my request.

Although it was a new strategy, his defiance told me we were in it for the long haul. I repeated my command, yet there was no luck. Heat permeated from behind and beads of moisture trickled down from my temple to my spine. *I was not giving up.* I changed my strategy.

"Tap head." I tapped my head, expecting him to imitate me. He struck the high chair tray and looked above.

I'd learned that attention and imitation skills were the basic elements to learning a skill. Before we learned to dance, we needed to observe others and follow their cue. The same method applied when learning a language. Gordon needed to master those skills. If he was stuck in his own world and refused to open his world to others, he would not learn that skill.

I repeated my command, raising my right hand to tap my head, while my left hand held his hand to follow.

"Good job, Gordon!" I presented him chips as his reward.

That caught his attention. A puzzled look crossed his face. If I could read his mind, Gordon must have thought, *"What are these chips for?"* He gobbled them right away.

In ABA terms, the assistance was called prompting, and the reward was called positive reinforcement. *Made sense...*

I gathered that the hand-over-hand assistance was foolproof. There was no way he could not comply. He should be able to accomplish the task with my hand on top of his. The intent was to fade the prompting until he responded appropriately and independently.

While we worked on our imitation skills with more tapping activity, I could conclude that our first day was more of a miss than a hit. The sweltering heat of a humid summer did not help motivate us to keep going. After thirty minutes, I gave up but vowed to carry on in the ensuing days. If that method could train sea lions, then it should work for Gordon. I spent that evening reading books, checking for finer points and strategies.

During the next few days, I modified the positive reinforcements, so they didn't lose their novelty and became ineffective to *force* the child to perform the task.

That time, instead of the edibles, I used his Matchbox car and allowed him to hold on to the car as we climbed up the stairs. By the time *work* was ready, I removed the car from his hands. Gordon planted his gaze on the car.

"Tap head," I ordered, but there was no response.

I repeated the gesture but this time with my assistance to tap his head. While he followed my cue, I handed him his Matchbox car and praised him. "Good job, now tap your shoulders, Gordon." I limited my language when praising him since his comprehension at that stage was still primitive. Few and repeated words would enable him to associate the word usage down the road.

He held on to the car for fifteen seconds before I took it from him.

We did our one-on-one sessions almost every weekday afternoon, at a minimum of thirty minutes to an hour, with Patrick participating at times, and soon Gordon got accustomed to the routine. Although the target behaviors were still to address attention and imitation skills, I would vary the approach and the prompting. For imitation skills, it could be a *tap nose* or *tap car* or *do this* while rubbing the nose or anything that could get him to follow me.

One afternoon, before I requested Gordon to do something, he opened his hand, an action which showed him asking for his reward. I wanted to jump for joy but reminded myself that it was a process, and we still had a long way to go. If the program was delivered in its rigid ways and with much intensity, I could spot changes in Gordon's behavior. I pretended to ignore his action and presented a request. He needed to understand that the reward was only given in response to a *good behavior.*

"Ma'am Leah?" A female voice intruded on my thoughts, and I realized I was at the airport, and Rose had arrived.

I studied the passport and other documents that she showed me which revealed the same pixie cut hairstyle and build. My guess as that she must be close to fifty years old. She spoke in a low, flat, mature voice which made me think she was quite levelheaded in contrast to an excitable voice of a flighty teenager.

Peace transcended over me. I knew Rose would be instrumental with Gordon's development. "Welcome to Canada, Rose. And just call me 'Leah.'"

FOURTEEN

"A sibling is the lens through which you see your childhood."

– Ann Hood

July 12, 1998

Far across the distance
And spaces between us
You have come to show you go on
Far across the distance...

The soundtrack from the movie *Titanic* played loudly on the radio, and it resonated with me, sensing how distant Gordon could be. Despite the situation, I knew my heart would go on.

The practice of staying up all night to craft our home program's first-week curriculum reminded me of college days studying for final exams. That time, however, instead of preparing to be tested, I was researching the various approaches on behavioral modification and determining how to incorporate them into Gordon's curriculum. I caught myself clasping my hands in a prayer gesture and smiling to myself. That program should make a positive difference in Gordon's development.

While Bingo worked in his home office in the basement and the boys were fast asleep in their bedrooms, I continued to work with no interruptions, hoping to create a full curriculum addressing Gordon's developmental delay, but I reminded myself to take it slow and start with simple, manageable tasks since that would be for the first week. The excitement and confidence I felt about the program that, I hope, would carve a path for Gordon's future fueled my energy. I had promised myself I would give the program my all.

The next day, I welcomed Marla and Charlie, the two people I just hired for my home program. I felt some vibration inside me as I studied their physical attributes. Marla, a Caucasian stay-at-home mother, wore a sundress. Charlie, who informed me during the interview that he had worked at the juvenile center dealing with the youth at risk, seemed to be a neat freak as he kept straightening his white T-shirt. Not a stray wrinkle could be found in his plaid Bermuda shorts, which likely had been pressed prior to his coming.

As I have indicated on the flyer, the job did not require work experience with children with autism. The books I had read warned me that some experienced workers may come with a preconceived approach to running the program. Without experience, I hoped they would be open and adaptable to the scripted curriculum for my son. My priority was to hire workers who possessed enthusiasm, which drove one's motivation to make a difference in one's work. I saw this enthusiasm and dedication in Marla and Charlie despite their inexperience working with children who have autism. My goal was to have a team of four, but with those two, I hoped we could balance the workload together.

We headed to the right side of the basement. "This is where you will work with Gordon, but we will hold our meetings over there." I pointed to the other side of the basement with the L-shaped sectional sofa upholstered with fuzzy brown material speckled with tiny white polka dots and led them over to our meeting place.

"Is that table upside down?" Marla asked in her soft, sweet, and doting tone, which reminded me of my aunt who was patient and allowed her children to express themselves.

"Yeah," I chuckled. "The table had a glass top, but we removed the glass to avoid accidents." She nodded in agreement.

I plopped into the corner of the sofa. Marla sat on the other end of the sectional sofa while Charlie rested on the chair. Our positions formed a triangle. Since it was our kick-off meeting where I would introduce a lot of topics that may be new to them, I'd opted to meet in the basement, so we didn't get distracted by the doorbells and telephone calls. "Thank you both for responding to my flyer." I started the meeting by handing out a two-page curriculum for the week. "We will have a one-hour paid meeting every Sunday at two in the afternoon."

Charlie bent forward to rest his forearms on his thighs while Marla crossed her legs and took notes. "In this basement is where all the work will take place," I paused and glanced at both of them. "Gordon may resist initially, but once this becomes a routine, he won't be too fussy about it. Rose, the caregiver I hired, will also be working with the both of you. Part of her role is to record the sessions while I review them in the evening."

Marla nodded slightly, grinning, while Charlie's eyebrows arched up and stayed there. They had not interrupted me. Both nodded once in a while.

Marla tied her hair in a ponytail while Charlie twiddled his fingers, eager to hear more about the program. "Before I get to the curriculum, let me share with you Gordon's developmental baseline. Gordon is four years and nine months old, yet he does not respond to his name. He appears not to hear us but has no hearing issues and acts like we don't exist. He walks through us like going through a glass pane."

They gasped. Marla looked like she was in deep thought while she covered her mouth with her hand. Charlie's eyes bulged like they were about to pop out.

I nodded to acknowledge their reaction. "He does not imitate, nor does he say *no*. Gordon has never addressed us as his parents." I enumerated the other developmental delays.

"He seemed cheerful when I was here last time," Charlie blurted out, not fully absorbing what he just heard. He leaned forward as he shook his head as if trying to process what he had just heard.

"Yes, he is a happy boy; unfortunately, that's where it all ends." I confirmed his observation while puckering my lips and shrugging my shoulders.

"I see," Marla said in a hushed tone while her hand covered her mouth.

"If you were to see photos of Gordon, you may not spot he has autism because he is just happy in his own world. He doesn't need to interact with other people to be happy. Individuals with autism have no physical manifestation of their diagnosis. They look perfectly normal, like you and me. Sad to say, that's what autism is all about."

As they made strong eye contact with me, I sensed their compassion. They seemed to want to get to know Gordon better, and they continued to take notes.

"Gordon's receptive skills is assessed to be equivalent to that of an eighteen-month-old, while his expressive skill matches a ten-month-old."

"What do you mean?" Charlie furrowed his eyebrows. I perceived that Charlie's line of work experience was different compared to what he'd be doing for me, but I appreciated his interest.

"An eighteen-month-old child understands a few words. When you tell the child to blow a kiss or show me beautiful eyes, he can act that out. Gordon does not."

"Why is that?" Marla spoke with the compassion of a doting mother. She shifted her weight and put both feet on the ground.

"I don't have answers to that, Marla. For me, it's an *autism* enigma. Why they are what they are and how they have become the way they are now, I don't know." I shook my head. My voice cracked, and tears welled up as I recalled my conversations with Dr. Bell, getting him to recognize the issue and pleading for him to refer us to a specialist. Focused on the purpose of the meeting, I tried to keep a straight face but couldn't ignore the butterflies in my stomach. As his mother, I felt I was to blame for the lack of assertiveness to have addressed his issues earlier. I had many wishes—wishing I did this and that—but life did not allow us to rewind time. The clock of life only moved forward.

"Gordon has been in the daycare for over eighteen months now. Prior to that, he was with a sitter who also took care of other children. You would think he would naturally imitate other children, eh?"

They nodded.

"What causes it?" Marla was curious. Her forehead revealed the creases as her gray eyes settled on me. She tapped her pen on her chin.

"There are many theories, but I've stopped following through on those. My urgent need now is to get Gordon to speak, call me *Mom*, say *No*, and enjoy our company."

Marla nodded with compassion written on her face. She seemed to want to hug me, feeling sorry for my situation.

"Okay, okay, I got it," Charlie said in an eager tone. He rubbed his hands. "What are we supposed to do? I am ready." He straightened his shoulders.

Swallowing hard, I wanted to tell them I lost so much hope when the doctors were nonchalant about Gordon's diagnosis and thought there was no other way, but I maintained my composure. Once they worked with Gordon, they would come to love him and do what was best.

From the basement, I heard the front door swing open and closed.

"Mom," Patrick yelled. "I'm home." He came running down to the basement.

"What happened, Pat?"

"Nothing." He shrugged. "We're done skating. Dad and Gordon are heading to the park. I told Dad I wanted to join your meeting."

He was only eight and a half years old but was sincere in helping his brother. A wide smile played on my lips, and I gave him a hug. *I was so proud of my boy.*

I introduced Patrick to Marla and Charlie. He sat beside me and stretched his legs, allowing them to dangle.

"Where was I?" I squinted my eyes and peeked at the paper in front of me, trying to recall the topic where we left off. "Oh, I remember. I am about to give you a background of the program." I paused then proceeded. "The program is called ABA, short for Applied Behavioral Analysis. The best comparison I can share for you to visualize this program is like how they train sea lions at Marine Land."

Their eyes grew wide.

"I am not making this up. There's a lot of research about this program on its efficacy for children with autism. The program follows an A-B-C paradigm." I gestured my hands in the air.

They listened and focused, not wanting to miss the important moment.

"A is for the antecedent or the request we give him; B is the behavior or his response he executes, and C is the consequence or the positive reinforcement, the reward he receives," I explained. "Hmm." I was not sure if I confused them with those buzzwords. "Perhaps we can roleplay, so I can best describe how this works."

They leaned forward.

"Please refer to the curriculum where it says to *do this ...while tapping your knees*. "Let's move to the other side where you will work with Gordon."

We rose and headed to where a child's table, chairs, and some bins could be found.

"Pat, come over here. Sit on this yellow chair." I sat on the blue chair, while Patrick followed instructions. Facing Charlie and Marla, I added, "It is important that you are within his eye level."

"Do this." I requested Patrick to tap his knees while maintaining eye contact.

As he emulated how Gordon would react to this command, Patrick ignored me, looked above, twirled his hands, and jumped on the sofa to the other side of the basement.

Marla and Charlie watched in amazement.

"What you witnessed today is very much what Gordon would do. He is being defiant." I chuckled, then faced Patrick. "Pat, you're such an actor." Then I faced them. "When that happens, you need to bring him back to this spot and continue with the process."

They both nodded in agreement.

Patrick settled into the chair. Then I repeated the command while hand-over-hand assisting him to tap his knees.

"Because of my assistance, which we call prompting, he is able to comply. Once that happens, you give him a reward, like chips."

Their eyes went wild.

"He'll be a junkie in this session." Charlie raised his hands in the air.

"That is if he complies all the time." I shrugged my shoulders and tilted my head. "He needs to relate that a reward is for the appropriate behavior, the correct response."

"Hmm." Charlie raised his eyebrows, and I presumed he had doubts, but like a teacher in a classroom, I ignored the disruptions and carried on with my lesson. After all, I was here to teach them.

"Let me digress here for a moment. Don't we all work to attain something?"

"What do you mean?" Charlie asked.

"Come on, Charlie. You didn't come here just because, did you?"

"Yeah, to have the extra income." He furrowed his eyebrows.

"The same thing. The extra income is your positive reinforcement. We all work for something. It's like we exercise to get fit. So, getting fit is our goal, our positive reinforcement. To put it another way, we exercise so we don't get fat. In other words, we work to avoid the negative consequence."

"That makes sense," Marla said. She seemed reserved in her ways, but I could sense that she got me, my point. Mothers thought alike, indeed.

"And when he does what we ask of him every time, the request becomes easy. When I see in the video that he's getting it all the time, I'll vary the curriculum, making it more challenging. But we start with easy requests."

"Is this our way of teaching him how to talk?" Marla leaned forward.

"There's a term for this, DTT which stands for Discrete Trial Teaching. It means teaching in structured and manageable steps. First, he needs to learn to imitate or to copy other people's ways. That's our 'Do this' instruction." I tapped my head.

Their nods reflected their attention and interest in the discussion.

"And if he cannot follow, we help him out, starting with the most intrusive way, like hand-over-hand assistance. We use our strategy of weaning him off that assistance to see if he can do it by himself. When he can execute independently, we generalize the skill. Let him imitate other things, like tap an object, imitate a sequence, imitate facial expressions. In these, he learns a lot by imitating. And when he knows how to imitate, a world of learning has opened up for him. Does that make sense?"

They both nodded and remained quiet. They must have been processing the thought that everything we learn started by imitating.

"What do you think?" I asked them while I also wondered if they were on board or skeptical. Butterflies flooded my stomach, and I hoped I was doing the right thing. Silence crossed between us as they reviewed the curriculum. I didn't want to overwhelm them with so much information, but that was one way of determining their dedication for this job.

We continued discussing the rest of the curriculum.

"Notice that I rewarded Pat for abiding by my request, but he was assisted. We need to wean him off that assistance." Charlie rubbed his clean-shaven chin, while Marla crossed her legs. Their eyes looked tired, but we were far from over.

We headed to the sofa where we were more comfortable.

"As I mentioned during your interviews, this is not a babysitting job. I have a sitter. Rose will be with Gordon. This is more like a teaching job." *The child was expected to follow to the tee, no ifs, ands, or buts from the child.*

"Yeah, it really sounds easy." Charlie straightened his shoulders with confidence. I loved his enthusiasm.

"I agree, it *sounds* easy, but remember, you have to contend with his behavior too."

"What do you mean?"

"Like what you saw earlier, he'll run away. He will refuse to cooperate with you."

"Okay, I got that," Charlie said.

"On teaching *No…*"

"Yeah, how do we teach that?" Charlie cut me off.

"Fortunately, we will use something we know he dislikes, and that's milk. Shortly after Gordon was diagnosed, he started throwing his cereal bowl or glass that was filled with milk. For some reason, and I haven't figured out why, he has associated milk as something that causes him discomfort."

"How do we teach that? For him to like milk?" Marla asked.

"No, not to like it, instead of spilling milk, he has to verbalize his dislike for it." I rose to reach for the toddler's sippy cup resting on the coffee table. "Before you start, Rose will fill this cup with milk. Present it to Gordon, then ask, 'Do you want milk?' He will most likely act up and shove the cup. Prompt him by having him say *No*, and when he can say that, provide the reward right away. Down the road, we will also remove the prompting, and he will need to respond on his own."

They nodded.

Moving forward, I checked the next section of our curriculum. "Point to family members." I showed them solo photos of our family and informed them that they needed to get Gordon to point at the photos when asked.

"He doesn't know that?" Marla raised her eyebrows. Being a mother of four, she must have been recalling her children's milestones.

"No, Marla, he doesn't. What others learn *naturally*, we are teaching him *deliberately*." I continued. "Gordon will not respond because he does not understand what you're asking him to do. Remember, his comprehension is at the level of an eighteen-month-old child. Get his hand and force him to point to Patrick's picture and reward immediately."

I explained to both of them that we had to start with simple and manageable requests then add two to three more photos to improve his receptive and understanding skills. "We have to teach him to understand something before he can express it. Down the road, maybe the next question would be, 'Who's that?' while pointing to the picture, and he will have to identify that as Patrick."

I assured them we shouldn't pressure ourselves and to start with something that was manageable.

"Rose will bring Gordon to the daycare in the afternoon, where he will have the opportunity to interact with other children." *That had really been my hope since he started in the daycare. Maybe with this intensive behavior modification home program, something would snap, and he would mingle with them.*

After our meeting, I led them upstairs to the kitchen where I served them rich, filled chocolate cupcakes that I baked earlier that day, hoping the sugar would lighten up the mood and prepare them for the next day.

While we were savoring our cupcakes, triumphant stories attributed to this program entered my thoughts. The emphasis on *early* intervention was the key to success, it had been noted. Sandra's daughter started this program when she was two and a half years old and so did the other children mentioned in the other books. I hadn't come across a success story of one who started at three years of age or older. There should be a story out there, or maybe no book was written about them. Gordon turned five in three months. I was storming heavens to help me narrow the distance between us which had compelled me to write this story.

As I bid my workers goodbye, Marla gave me a tight hug which helped me ease my worries, while Charlie pumped his fist in the air like we had won an Oscar award. I stared at the sky above and noticed that the sky was clear, reminding me to cherish new beginnings.

FIFTEEN

"Nothing in this world can take the place of persistence. Talent will not: nothing is more common than unsuccessful men with talent.

Genius will not; unrewarded genius is almost a proverb. Education will not: the world is full of educated derelicts. Persistence and determination alone are omnipotent."

- Calvin Coolidge

July 17, 1998

Basking in the natural light streaming inside the living room while waiting for Charlie and Marla for our weekly team meeting, I allowed myself to get lost in my thoughts. My made-up movie title, *My Week That Was*, was playing in my mind as I reviewed and critiqued each scene.

I rushed the boys to bed last Monday night to give myself ample, quality time in reviewing the videos Rose took of the session that day. It didn't take long for my excitement to be derailed when I saw that the sessions were not conducted as I had hoped they would be. I made notes in our logbook to remind Charlie and Marla of my ways of handling Gordon, hoping they would amend their ways and deliver as I had envisioned. But the following sessions that Tuesday and the remaining days of the week were somewhat the same. *They were not getting it.*

By Thursday, I snapped at Bingo which caught him by surprise. Startled, he was awoken after dozing off while watching TV, since the instant bark came with no warning. While reviewing this made-up movie in my mind, I realized now that emotions had crammed in my chest. First, my home program had not gone as smoothly as I had expected it to. Secondly, I was reminded of Bingo's skepticism about the home program. Although Bingo and I were now convinced that autism was causing Gordon's odd behavior, we had not been on the same page on how to intervene despite agreeing on our lack of confidence in the professionals' approach. He reminded me that through the eighteen months that Gordon had been seeing those professionals, he still had not learned to call our name. "Are you sure you know what you're going to do?"

No, I was never sure I knew what I would do. Who did? Would my program teach him to call us by our names? I couldn't guarantee that.

The only guarantee in life was that it was full of uncertainties. Monkey wrenches would always be thrown in our paths. I believed as long as we had a direction and a strong desire to get to the finish line, we would be able to handle those monkey wrenches, and slowly but surely, we would forge ourselves to some forward direction. But nothing begot anything, and something begot something.

Embarking into this uncharted territory neither of us was trained for was making Bingo insecure. I understood that. Our mathematics training taught us analytical skills where every theory needed to be proven.

"What harm will that do to him, anyway? We're not medicating him," I reasoned out. Despite his lukewarm attitude toward the home program, I proceeded as planned because deep in my heart, I knew this would work.

How I wished we had been mandated to take up a subject of psychology in the university to help us understand behaviors. After all, we would always be dealing with behaviors with our family and with everyone we meet. But I digressed. I would have to plow through on my own.

Although sunshine uplifted my spirits, my emotions were like a kettle filled with water reaching its boiling temperature. I could feel the hot water bubbling inside me. I would need to ignore the bubbling inside me and listen to Charlie and Marla's challenges and address them the best way I knew how, for Gordon's sake.

Taking a deep breath, I welcomed the day ahead, hoping for a productive day.

As soon as we reached the basement, Marla scanned the curriculum while Charlie straightened the collar of his polo shirt.

"We survived the first week, eh? What did you think?" I tried to break the ice.

Silence crossed between us.

Charlie cleared his throat. "I understood our discussion last week but didn't expect him to be defiant. He refused to listen."

Loud thuds emerged from my chest.

Charlie continued. "I was about to spank his behind, but Rose stopped me."

"Excuse me?" My eyes widened.

"Why can't we do that?" He gestured his hand in the air as Italians did. I recalled that his real name was Carlo but as a young immigrant boy, he preferred to be called Charlie to avoid being teased. "I don't mean a hard spank. Like, when he turned the table, I wanted to spank his hand. That's what we do at work, I mean to these older children."

From the video, I could visualize the scene he was referring to. I had anticipated this suggestion. I would think that at Charlie's workplace, disciplining the delinquents would be harsh. But the delinquents, I suppose, were repeat law offenders and were able to verbally articulate, unlike Gordon.

"No, no, no," I cut him off before he could provide more examples. "We're not tolerating physical discipline here. There is zero tolerance for that. In school, that's what they call a no-touch policy."

"But that is effective. No pain, no gain," Charlie rested his hands on his hips. "You're just spoiling him. As they say, life is not a bed of roses."

As I observed Charlie, I thought that maybe his work experience was impacting his sessions with Gordon.

"No," I raised my voice, sounding more adamant in my attempt to muffle his argument. "It has been said that positive reinforcement is five times more effective than negative reinforcement."

His facial expression was like a reflection of a distorted mirror often found in amusement parks. "That's just in the books. What do you mean? How?"

My head spun as I paced the room. There was no way I could work with someone who wanted to spank my child. However, if I let Charlie go, he could do that to someone else's child. It needed to be addressed now. Taking a deep breath, said, "Had you spanked him for toppling over the table, Gordon would have stopped for that moment *only*."

Charlie puckered his lips and shook his head in disbelief.

"When the pain is gone, he will test your limits and act up again. That's what a negative reinforcement does. It is short-lived." I paused to check their reaction. I checked on Marla's facial expression. I felt like 'mothering' her despite her being older than me.

"When you deprive a kid of something, he will find ways to retrieve it." I continued, not waiting for a reaction from them. "The urge to reclaim what they want is powerful, but with positive reinforcement, he can learn, and once he does, it is permanent. As part of the program, we work on varying those positive reinforcements. Our goal is that he sees a high five or an ecstatic *wow* as reinforcements worth working for. Isn't that the way we are? A smile in our mother's face is worth our hard work at school?" I heaved a sigh. I felt like I had given a lecture. How could I make this interesting?

They didn't say a word.

"Back in school, when you got good marks after working hard on your exam, didn't you feel good? Acquiring good grades motivates you to work harder, similar to the brownie points."

The stillness continued to make me uneasy. I wondered what Marla had to say. "Marla, how was your experience?"

"He does not want to work," Marla blurted out. "He brought the table down." She demonstrated how Gordon knocked down the table.

"Based on the video, I noticed that you kept coaxing him, but there's no need for too much talking; please stick to the script."

"I read your note, but why do we have to follow the script? Isn't that *unnatural?*" The inflection of her tone spelled exasperation.

I wondered if both Charlie and Marla would be here for the long haul. It had only been the first week, and they couldn't seem to handle Gordon. "What do you mean?" My voice cracked up. She tried to be calm, but something told me that Marla didn't agree with the method. My breathing was rapid, yet I tried my best to keep my composure, so I could capture every word she said.

"And do you know why Gordon is the way he is?" She paused while I maintained my silence. The truth was, I didn't want to know why. Marla's eyes were guarded as she shook before speaking. "Because you don't have the warmth of a loving mother, Leah."

"I'm sorry?" Heat permeated my cheek, and I knew my blood pressure had risen. Words didn't, couldn't escape my lips. In other words, she supported the old theory that children with autism were a result of a stone-hearted mom.

Marla leaned forward "My children grew up without going through this nonsense."

With that powerful statement, my gaze froze on the vibrant colors of the ethnic tapestry above the sofa where they remained glued as I took deep breaths, reminding myself that they were here to help me out. I couldn't afford to lose them, not at this time.

Continuing to be professional, I faced them both. "Gordon's comprehension is limited. He does not pick up language like a typical kid. We need to address Gordon by his first name and not using terms of endearment. Have you ever wondered why your children are able to talk without going through this nonsense?"

Marla shook her head while Charlie listened.

"That's because they don't have autism, but my son does."

A wave of silence filled the air.

I couldn't contain my emotions and excused myself to head to our bedroom where I curled up like a ball and exploded into tears. Bingo appeared moments later carrying a dozen roses with Gordon and Patrick hovering around me. Tears spilled from my eyes, but that time it was due to joy. *This was my family. We may never be normal, but we strived to do our best.*

SIXTEEN

"By holding the highest vision for your child when they can not see it for themselves, you are lifting them up, elevating them and helping them to soar."

– Megan Koufos

August 1998

After coming to terms with Marla's statement, I spent the next meeting explaining to them the different strategies on how to deal with an autistic child. Marla apologized to me, and I explained to both of them positive reinforcements and the importance of being an authoritative teacher who was in control.

"Gordon will need to respond the same way as the command is given by various people with different personalities. As part of my team, you are a representation of the teachers he will have in his lifetime. Some of you may speak in a monotonous tone while others reveal more enthusiasm; Gordon's reaction should be the same."

They stared at me as if they were trying to process some words of wisdom.

"Isn't this reward system the same as bribery? What's the difference?" A puzzled look crossed Marla's face.

"What you did, Marla, is bribery. You enticed him to do something by showing the reward."

This time, all eyes were glued to me.

"Positive reinforcement is spontaneous. Something like a token of appreciation for a job well done."

From the looks on their face, I still didn't sound convincing, but I couldn't give up.

We discussed the upcoming curriculum, a variation of the first week. We didn't need to go through the details that time. "Remember, besides imitation skills, we are also targeting other skills like comprehension, compliance, attention, listening, and other skills."

"Wow," Marla whispered to herself. And in a more audible voice, she added, "I guess I didn't realize that."

***

No setback wavers my commitment to my family. In my prayers, I continued to ask God for strength, guidance in this journey, and good health. I knew the program would work; I kept reminding myself of that despite all the challenges I faced.

At seven o'clock in the evening on a Friday night, while Bingo took the boys out to the nearby park, I was working on next week's program in my office in the corner of our master bedroom. With a can of Coke and determined to complete the program, I was prepared to pull an all-nighter.

Dr. Lovaas, the pioneer of ABA, stressed the importance of early intervention and intensity for a remarkable gain in a child's development. While four and a half years old was no longer considered early, I could only work with the parameters that were within my control and hope for the best.

The other key factor was the quality of the therapy session. *Quality*? Who was to say that had we gone with Autism Services, the sessions would be of better quality and more effective? Not being in two places at the same time was an unfortunate fact of life. Had Autism Services developed Gordon's program, could Gordon have made more gains? As I had familiarized myself with ABA and DTT concepts, I introduced them to Charlie and Marla in our kick-off meeting, and understanding the functions of behavior, it had to be a blessing in disguise that I was forced to develop and manage Gordon's program.

No one knew Gordon and his idiosyncrasies as much as I did. I knew what tickled and annoyed him and how to leverage those to get him to respond. The application of the generic curriculum presented in the books to tailor fit Gordon's needs was something I believed I could do more effectively than others. However, anyone who hired other people to take care of their son should still be involved in the program's development.

I closed my eyes, trying to recall ideas that flashed through my mind while I tapped the Coke can with the edge of the pen. Patrick popped into our bedroom, reminding me I had been mulling over the curriculum for over an hour now.

"Hi, Mom." He planted a kiss on my cheek.

"Where are Dad and Gordon?"

"They're in the backyard. It's hot out there." In that part of the world, the sun showed its weariness sometime around nine thirty.

"I think you need to take a shower," I said and wrinkled my nose as I wiped the sweat off his shirt.

He grinned and exited the bedroom.

Ever since I had immersed myself in Gordon's program, I often thought of Patrick and his need for my attention and longing for a brotherly bond with Gordon. It must have been last year, 1997, when we last partied with other friends with kids of my boys' age. But in recent months, I had not thought of reaching out to them, and whenever they did, I could no longer give our conversations the excitement I used to. *Nothing excited me as much as ABA those days, but I couldn't tell them that.*

It would have been convenient for Patrick to just stay home during the summer and do whatever he wanted since Rose and Gordon were at home, but that would not be good use of his time. Instead, I opted for Patrick to attend a summer day camp at a nearby public school. At least he was occupied with something and got to hang out with kids his age. Now in his PJs, Patrick settled on the chair beside me, dangling his feet and tucking his hands under his thighs.

"What's the program like this week, Mom? Anything new?"

Patrick had been joining me at the meetings. After his summer camp, he rushed down to the basement to observe Gordon's session. He was like an adult who cared for the welfare of Gordon.

I turned the desktop computer CRT monitor toward him and pointed to the program on the screen.

"More imitation, but this time with the sequence imitation. I think the perfect sequence will be the sign of the cross. Two steps, followed by three, then four.

And also, more colors, shapes, and numbers recognition."

"Mom, can I be Gordon's worker too?"

At eight years old, I wasn't sure if he really meant what he said. *Gordon's worker?* It might look easy to teach, but could he handle the tantrums? However, the tone of Patrick's voice sounded like he longed for that brotherly love. He must envy his classmates' interactions with their siblings.

"You mean you want to have a session with Gordon?" I nodded and wiggled my forefinger close to my temple. "Hmm. You know what… we can all be Gordon's workers."

"Huh?" Patrick arched his eyebrows.

"Giving the commands does not have to be in a scheduled session. We can do that. When he's playing with his car, for example." I paused, waiting for him to react, but a puzzled look crossed his face.

"You don't join him in that kind of play. It's not fun, right?"

He nodded.

"His kind of play makes little sense. It's back and forth. It's no fun. It's a *stim*, that's what they call it, Pat. *Stim*," I repeated to emphasize the word that would soon be a common word not only to our family but with the autism community. "This repetitive nonsense activity is called *stim*. We need to help him stop that *stim*, or at least lessen it."

"But we already tried that. We hid those cars, re-member? Then he goes around and grabs another thing and *stims* with it."

"*Just* taking away those cars won't help. When we remove something so dear to him, he will find a way to get that back. If he can't find it, he will replace it with something. It will be the same *stim* activity but with a different object. And if he can't find a replace-ment, he'll throw a tantrum."

"That's what I said. Then what? What's the plan?"

"When he's stimming with that object, take it, hold on to it, quickly give him a command, and have him imitate you just like what we do in the sessions." I purposely spoke slow to allow him to visualize the steps. He was following, I could tell.

"The first time you give him the command, you'll need to assist him, and since he will respond accurate-ly, the reward needs to be given right away."

He nodded, processing what I said.

"There was a time when I thought he was expect-ing a reward. We need to get him to respond appro-priately all the time. He needs to crave that reward."

"I get it. That sounds like a game. How do we stop him *stimming*?" He stretched his legs.

I realized I had digressed so much. "You see, the longer he is *stimming* by himself, the stronger the pull is to his *nether*world, where he is distant from us. He is contented and happy in his own world."

I had been so wrapped up in my conversation with Patrick that I failed to witness the sunset. The sun was gone to his *nether*world. Darkness crept in, but I knew the sun would be back. My voice cracked. My beautiful baby, Gordon, needed to come back to his family. I cleared my throat, reminding myself my ally, Patrick, was here to help. *We were a strong team, and we could do this.*

"What do you mean, pull to what world?"

"He enjoys his *alone* time. We want him to have fun being with us, so we need to intervene when Gordon does his nonsense."

Before I realized it, it was almost midnight when Bingo and Gordon entered the room.

"Hey Dad. We have a new house rule," Patrick said.

Bingo eyed him then affixed his gaze on me. "What do you mean?"

"Intervene with Gordon at all times, especially when he is *stimming.*"

While Patrick explained to Bingo what needed to be done, I closed my eyes and took a deep breath. *It was a work in progress. I was getting there, my dear.* I looked up at Bingo and gave him a big hug.

SEVENTEEN

*"Until you have a kid with special needs you have
no idea of the depth of your strength, tenacity
and resourcefulness."*

– Anonymous

September 1998

Charlie and Marla left us after summer ended,
and I presumed that they only needed a summer job. Since the program recommended
having a minimum team of four workers, I now had
three workers: Ayesha, a senior in high school and a
practicing Muslim who wore a hijab, Ana, a psychology student at the University who was referred to us by
a mutual friend, and Miguel who was a junior in high

school, also referred to us. So far, I was happy that they were following my scripts to the tee. Gordon seemed to be comfortable working with them and didn't run away from the scene. However, I couldn't discount the possibility that Gordon was more used to the routine now, two months since we started.

With Rose taking the weekend off, there was no taping today. Patrick and I sat at the bottom of the stairs, observing the workers.

It was Ayesha's turn to work with Gordon. Based on my observation, even at the height of summer, Ayesha's religion required that she cover her arms and legs, along with wearing a hijab. Unlike Marla and Charlie, Ayesha struck me as reserved. During meetings, she was usually quiet, which I initially thought to be attributed to her inexperience working with a child. After several sessions with Gordon, I observed that Ayesha kept opinions about the program or Gordon's behavior to herself before bringing it up to me. *I liked her; she was giving this program a chance.* Glancing at her notes, Ayesha ran her finger on the page to check the next drill and required materials.

While perched on the chair, Gordon watched Ayesha lay down a flash card with a red balloon and another card with a green square, the materials for the first trial. In her pleasant voice, she said, "Touch color red."

Gordon didn't budge, so Ayesha assisted him in touching the flash card with the red balloon.

"Good, touch red, Gordon," Ayesha praised Gordon and rewarded him with two cheerios.

For the second trial, Ayesha replaced the flashcards with the Thomas the blue train and James the red train from the Thomas the Tank Engine train set.

"Mom, he could do that on his own yesterday," Patrick whispered, feeling dismayed.

She repeated her command. "Touch color red." She raised her eyebrows while keeping an eye on Gordon to make a move then nodded a few times.

Gordon ignored the command, looked up, and swayed his head from left to right. Ayesha reached out to his elbow with a light touch and guided his forearm.

With assistance, Gordon's hand landed on James the red train.

"Good, touch red, Gordon," Ayesha praised him with more enthusiasm that time.

Patrick glanced at Gordon from his peripheral vision. It might not have been his brother's response that pleased him, but more of Gordon's attention and compliance.

For the third trial, Ayesha replaced the trains with a flash cards with a blue balloon, a red ball, and a yellow sippy cup, spaced six inches apart.

"Touch color red." Ayesha tapped Gordon's elbow and released her hand right away to see if Gordon would comply on his own.

With his behavior today, we needed to take advantage of this learning moment. Afraid that a slight sound may distract Gordon, I cupped my mouth. I couldn't let my breathing be heard. Inside me, I was cheering, '*Come on, Gordon, you can do it.*' Patrick and I never once batted an eyelash since we couldn't miss the big moment.

His hand moved over one object to the other, and as soon as it hovered over the red ball, Gordon eyed Ayesha, seemingly asking for a cue.

Seeking Ayesha's assistance using eye contact was a huge step; he felt the need for another human being. That was good.

Ayesha raised both her eyebrows and nodded, signaling him to land his hand on that object.

As soon as his hand landed on the red ball, we rose. Patrick raised his fists in the air and gave the loudest cheer as if Gordon had just made a touchdown. "Yeah, Gordon. You got it."

"Good job. Go play." Ayesha rewarded him with a short break from the session.

Gordon dashed over to the corner of the basement and jumped over the sofa. His facial expression remained pleasant. He showed neither pride nor a sense of accomplishment for his 'touchdown.'

Patrick and I approached Gordon to give him a high five. While Ayesha tidied up, I stepped outside the house and spotted a vibrant rainbow staring right back at me. The colors were bursting with character. I studied my surroundings, checking if anyone was around, but there was nobody. A tiny giggle mixed with tears escaped my lungs as I swayed my hips. *That felt so good.* Seeing Gordon engaged with Ayesha today only proved that the best things happen when we were patient. I was aware that we had a long way to go, but I was basking with hope and knew it wouldn't let me down.

***

In the kitchen, I scooped the last rasher of bacon from the pan to the serving dish. The sound of Bingo's heavy footsteps startled me.

"What's going on here?" Bingo adjusted his eyeglasses and studied the kitchen wall. He spotted labels and colored pictures taped to the walls leading to the basement which now resembled a kindergarten classroom.

Upon occupying this house fourteen months ago, we'd been very careful not to have a dent, a scratch on the wall, nor a peeling paint. When we moved furniture, Bingo had always reminded us to be extra careful, maybe until we learn the tricks of a handyman. The only frames on the walls were those I hung using thumbtacks.

"I am trying to get your son back to us," I raised my pitch a tad with a tone of sarcasm. I realized it was not a response he expected on this gorgeous Saturday morning, but I didn't have the energy to explain my strategy to him today. Since embarking on the home program, I had been in constant search of different approaches to help Gordon. *I wondered if he was getting impatient that he still had not seen results.* I reminded Bingo about our new house rule of intervening with Gordon, especially when he's stimming, and then I added, "And every minute of his waking time."

For the actual command, Gordon was expected to respond the same way regardless of the setting, be it in the session or outside the session, like at home, in the car, or in the park.

After completing the draft of Gordon's program for the upcoming week at three o'clock that morning, my work pager went off. I told the computer operator I'd get back to them in an hour and only remembered that promise now at eight o'clock this morning. I dropped and dozed off after that call. *Oh well, I hoped they were able to reach out to the secondary on-call person.* The truth was I dreaded the thought of driving to work at that unholy hour and hoped I could resolve the issue over the phone.

Last night, Bingo reminded me that fall was here.

"Are we sending Gordon to school this time?" I asked for a few more months of extension. That question went unresolved last night. I was sure he did not appreciate my response earlier and its tone. He shrugged his shoulders, rolled his eyes, and let the issue be. Bingo removed the eggs from the refrigerator to prepare breakfast.

I scooted upstairs to get Gordon ready for his session that morning. As we strolled down, we faced the colorful wall with my taped labels and colored pictures.

"Touch color red." I surprised him with the command, and with my hand over his hand, we touched the picture of a red fire truck.

"Good job. Now touch color red, Gordon." I shrieked in delight despite his assisted response.

As we stepped inside the kitchen, and I summoned him to touch the stove in the same manner and praised him afterward.

I did not need to present him a tangible positive reinforcement in those casual settings. Proceeding to where he was going, to the breakfast area in this case, was a reward.

Patrick, now seated in the breakfast nook, bent over to give Gordon a high five. "Yeah, Gordon." Patrick's cheer could not be undermined because he brought a ray of sunshine.

"Mom, you have to watch today's session. Gordon's almost getting it."

Although I had already seen the video last night, there was nothing like seeing it live with Patrick.

Patrick's enthusiasm was contagious. Gordon couldn't help but force a smile on his poker face, followed by a roar of laughter. Patrick, Bingo, and I joined in the laughter. For one moment, the natural chemicals being released from my body surged my spirits. It was easy to forget that forcing Gordon to respond had brought us so much joy and working together as a family created synergy.

After breakfast, Gordon ran upstairs then appeared moments later with a light blanket around his head.

Bingo glared at me. "What's with the blanket?" Then facing Gordon, he said, "Put that back. You don't drag a blanket around the house."

"Hush." With my forefinger on my lips, I whispered, "Don't you get it?"

He arched his right eyebrow and tilted his head.

"He's imitating without being told. He's wearing the blanket like Ayesha's hijab," I said.

"Hmm." He sighed.

"Let him be," I add. "For now."

My faith soared, my adrenaline was racing, and my heart was full. *I just might have latched on to the glimmer of the hope rope.*

EIGHTEEN

"[Autism is] appreciating the small things that some people might not understand and that, in itself, can show people the general beauty of things"

– IndieAndy: Autism Advocate

October 1998

As fall announced its arrival with the vibrant colors of the falling leaves, I was reminded of Shelley's prediction that Gordon would either be mute or speak in a robotic manner. Although it had been a year since I heard those lines, her statement was a difficult pill to swallow.

However, to this day, Gordon had never called me *Mom,* and he still could not verbalize his needs.

I couldn't bear the thought that Shelley's prediction would become a reality. I lay awake at night wondering what lay beneath his future—*our future.*

As we watched the World Series baseball game on TV, I asked Bingo, "Do you think Gordon will ever speak?"

"Hush," he brushed me away, his eyes glued to the TV. Baseball used to be a big part of our lives. We would share with friends the circumstances of Gordon's birth, that he came earlier than scheduled because of my excitement watching the Blue Jays clinch the title.

How could he be more interested in the game when Gordon's fifth birthday was next week?

Trying a different strategy to capture Bingo's attention, I said, "I might as well cancel Gordon's birthday party." The last thing I wanted to do was cancel my son's birthday party, but my patience was wearing thin.

Bingo bolted upright. He gave me his undivided attention. "Why?"

I pursed my lips. "I want to check Eden Institute in New Jersey for their behavior modification program."

I had always been confident of my next move, but that time, my enthusiasm wasn't there.

Bingo turned off the TV and inched closer, sensing that my hope was dwindling and I was in dire need of ideas to incorporate into our home program, which I hoped would prompt Gordon to talk.

Silence crossed between us. We both knew that Gordon's condition had taken a toll on our family. I had immersed myself in the program for the past three months where *I ate, breathed, lived the program.* We had deprived our family of summer outings since we started the program, so a trip to New Jersey would be a breather for all of us.

Without seeking further details, Bingo gave me a thumbs-up.

I hoped someday Gordon would understand that helping him learn to speak was worth canceling his fifth birthday party.

***

The long van ride to New Jersey didn't erase the guilt I bore for canceling Gordon's fifth birthday party, but I reminded myself that we needed to go to Eden Institute to check out their behavior modification program which would benefit him. Although we had traveled several times to New Jersey where my sister lived, I was still unsure how Gordon felt about the long trip.

Autism was defined by unpredictable behavior. And because he was still non-verbal, we could never be sure when he was okay with the decisions we made for him.

Ensuring that everyone was comfortable, Bingo hummed a tune behind the wheel, while I checked on Patrick and Gordon who were both seated at the back.

Butterflies formed in my stomach. I hoped the behavioral modification would work.

"Hey, Gordon." I snapped my fingers. His eyes were glued to the colorful foliage of upstate New York. "Gordon." I studied how he craned his neck to eye the road in front of us.

He glanced to the left window to witness cars passing by. Patrick drifted off to sleep. Not once did his brother shut his eyes during that seven-hour drive. He must have enjoyed the long ride. I couldn't believe he was five years old, yet his fascination for cars had never dwindled.

***

Eden Institute was closer to my cousin's place in Cherry Hill, New Jersey. I had suggested to Bingo we drop by their place in case they were home, so I could introduce them to my family. As we drove by their neighborhood, I gushed at how the trees had matured with leaves forming like a canopy on the road. I used to visit this place fifteen years ago when her kids were as young as my sons were today. I recalled the two-story colonial homes in that neighborhood, but they now looked more modern compared to before.

By luck, my cousin, Ramon, his wife Arlene, and one of their two children were home. They invited us inside their beautiful home, and we settled in their kitchen.

We updated Ramon and Arlene about Gordon's autism diagnosis and our home program. Ramon rose to fetch a tray of cookies and water. They also shared the developments of their three children. While we caught up on our lives, their eighteen-year-old son, who is deaf-mute, spent time in the basement with Patrick and Gordon.

"Nice of you to have dropped by. But what brings you to our neck of the woods?" Ramon popped a cookie in his mouth.

I mentioned that we had come down here to visit Eden Institute to check out their curriculum we planned to incorporate into our home program.

"Gordon's responses are still assisted in many ways. He has not learned to make his wants known. When we catch him with his knees together, bending while wiggling, we ask if he needs to go to the washroom." Bingo offered to give them a quick description of Gordon's mannerisms.

Arlene took a sip of water. As an anesthesiologist, I wondered if she had seen many children with autism.

Being with family helped me to open up more. "He does not ask for help from anyone. It's like we're ghosts. When Gordon is in the kitchen helping himself to the cupboard for a glass, we stop him by taking the glass and only give it back if he attempts to ask for our help."

"Does that strategy work?" Creases formed in her forehead. With a medical profession, Arlene was most likely aware of how autistic people behaved but preferred to keep her opinion to herself.

Tears welled up as I recalled what I thought before Gordon received his diagnosis. *Why did deaf-mute individuals have the sense to ask for assistance, while my son could not?*

I explained to them how we fill every minute of Gordon's waking time with a teaching opportunity, like while walking up the stairs, before brushing his teeth, while getting dressed, and before getting into the car, among other times.

"We verbalize everything we do with him and quiz him at random," I added. "And when he gets it right, we exaggerate our kudos. We make a big deal out of it, so he knows it was the right response." I turned to Bingo and continued. "Bingo has evolved to becoming an eager teacher who gives the loudest cheer. Boisterous cheer, I have to add." I chuckled and turned to them.

They nodded. From the puzzled looks on their faces, they seemed to visualize a snippet of our day.

As I shared my family situation, I realized that we had not had a conversation with anyone who knew much about autism until now. Even if the subject was still about autism, there was a great sense of relief in getting it off my chest. I hoped one day we would be normal and be able to do things that other families did, but right now, we were clouded with shades of gray.

"And how has this approach been playing out for him?" She rose from her seat to pile the dishes in the sink.

Before I could respond to Arlene, her son appeared from the basement and communicated in sign language to his parents.

Arlene peered at me then back at her son. Ramon's eyes were guarded, and he couldn't seem to look at me.

A knot formed in my stomach. "Is everything okay?" I was concerned that something unfortunate might have happened in the basement.

Arlene and Ramon exchanged glances and didn't say a word.

"Please," I begged.

She pursed her lips. "My son asked if the little boy downstairs is also deaf and mute."

The room spun as tears trickled down my cheeks. I covered my eyes, knowing *we were far from over.*

NINETEEN

"Autism Community: Where we cheer on each other's loved ones to succeed as much as our own. Every milestone is a celebration."

– Kerry Magro

October 1998

Our trip to New Jersey was quite a respite and a breather for us. Since it was also my nephew's birthday a few days before Gordon's, my sister got two cakes, one for each boy to blow out their candles on.

As I perused the materials of new ideas, I learned from the curriculum manuals purchased from Eden Institute, I was again seeing a glimmer of hope.

Though the glimmers came in trickles, they were enough to keep me on the upswing. Armed with those glimmers of hope, I was filled with the optimism of the likelihood that Gordon could adjust to the school environment in January, only two months away.

From the Eden Institute material, I would incorporate the kindergarten curriculum into his home program. And whatever he would learn in school, we would reinforce at home. The behavior modification program, which emphasized intensity as the key to learning and mastery, supported the cliché that practice made us better at what we did.

Often, in my excitement, I forgot that Gordon could not carry a conversation. He still babbled to himself all the time. I refused to allow my thoughts to dwell on what he couldn't do but focus on what he could do and build from there. Didn't the building block of learning start with what we already knew?

Since his diagnosis, Gordon had been seeing Claire, Dr. Pelletier's appointed speech and language therapist who worked for the government. During every visit, Claire sent us a pre-printed homework sheet that appeared to be one approach for all her patients. As I learned more about behavior modification, I was losing confidence in Claire's approach and its efficacy to get Gordon to communicate. But we continued to see her since there were no better options at the moment.

Shortly after we returned from New Jersey, Bingo suggested that we consult with Tricia, a speech and language pathologist who worked for a private firm.

"How did you hear about her?" I asked.

"Do you remember Sandra, the one who introduced us to this ABA program?" He paused, waiting for me to acknowledge my recollection. "I met someone at work who knows Sandra. They're seeing Tricia for their son, too."

There was nothing like seeing a professional who had been tried, tested, and highly recommended by someone who trekked in a similar path.

Although Bingo had not been keen about the home program, he had not opposed it either. Without being vocal about it, Bingo seemed to give the approach a chance before he was a hundred percent on board. Our conversation with my cousin and his wife in New Jersey, and sensing their compassionate reaction, must have been an eye-opener for Bingo. Plus, the blanket incident last month could also be a validation that we were making some progress. Bingo now shared our family situation and developments with his coworkers, neighbors, and friends. *Bingo was on board. We were all on board.*

Instead of our usual home program today, Katie, a tall, plump lady that exudes authority, was sent by Tricia to our home to introduce us to PECS—Picture Exchange Communication System—aimed at teaching Gordon to have the initiative to verbalize his needs.

Patrick, Gordon, Katie, and I formed a circle on the Berber carpet in our basement. Gordon sat right across from Katie who laid down her materials she pulled from her bag. *She was organized and came prepared.* Three vertical Velcro strips were glued on the blank photo album page. Attached to the Velcro strips were laminated pictures: a picture of a car, a mandarin orange, and a train. She also had a laminated yellow Bristol board with a strip of Velcro which she called the sentence strip. Katie informed us that when Gordon wanted something, he was supposed to grasp the picture from the photo album, attach it to the sentence strip, and hand it over to Katie.

Unsure what PECS was all about, I expressed my doubt. "But we are already doing the ABA program. He might get confused."

"Perfect," she said with glee. "No need to worry because you can integrate this into your program."

Katie took the red Matchbox car from Gordon, then guided him to select a picture of the car while helping him attach the photo to the sentence strip.

Defiant as expected when something new was introduced to him, Gordon threw away the materials.

Without a word, Katie persisted by picking up the supplies and repeating the process. As soon as the picture was attached to the sentence strip and handed to her, Katie gave Gordon the car. "Car, Gordon?" she said with enthusiasm. "Here you go."

Katie went through several iterations of this exercise until Gordon picked up the habit of what needed to be done. *I wished I had recorded that to show to my workers. When Gordon misbehaved, without any cooing, she got him back on track. She was in control of the session. She was firm.*

PECS was such a breath of fresh air. Right in front of my eyes, I witnessed Gordon responding to Katie. My body froze. *It was working.* How to incorporate PECS into our home program and apply it to our day-to-day activities flooded through my mind. I was geared up to get this application going.

After Katie concluded her session with Gordon, I was ecstatic about the potential of what the program had to offer, and I informed the daycare manager.

The sight of Gordon interacting with Katie only proved he was receptive and teachable, and the PECS method works.

***

Labels of our names, *Dad, Mom, Patrick,* and *Gordon* were attached to the chairs of the breakfast table to indicate our assigned seats. After Katie's session yesterday, I went to Scholastics Choice, a teacher's store for their visual aids, materials, and books to purchase huge picture books which our nanny, Rose, used to cut and laminate family, food, and toy photos into a twenty-page album.

I had witnessed the progress in Gordon when he brought the photo album to the dining room and leafed through the pages like he was studying a restaurant menu.

After choosing what he wanted, Gordon took the picture from the page, attached it to the sentence strip, and gave it to us. If his expressive skill was assessed at ten months old two years ago, this was a milestone, albeit at five years old.

Seated at our respective chairs for breakfast, Patrick drilled Gordon.

"Who's that?" he asked, pointing to Bingo. "Say, Dad."

After several repetitions, Gordon said, "Dada." Patrick continued to quiz him, and shortly after, Gordon responded me *Mama* followed by *Pepe* for Patrick and *Goge* for Gordon.

A warm sensation washed over me. *He had finally called me Mama. Hope existed after all.*

Now that Gordon had established our names, the next step would be for him to get our attention.

While having breakfast, Bingo hid Gordon's bacon but left two rashers on his plate.

Silence filled the air as we waited for his reaction.

Gordon eyed us, but we tried to keep a straight face. He fiddled with his rice without complaint.

"What's wrong, Gord?" Patrick spoke up.

Without hesitation, Gordon scooped up some of Patrick's bacon.

Bingo grasped his hands. "Gordon, say *bacon, please.*"

Patrick rose from his seat and dashed over to the living room to fetch the photo album. Upon his return, he showed Gordon a picture of how bacon looks.

With Patrick's assistance, Gordon attached the picture to the same sentence strip and handed over the sentence strip to Bingo.

We all watched in awe of the progress he had made. My heart leapt. *That was my boy!*

"Bacon." Bingo beamed. "Here you go. Bacon." Then he gave Gordon the bacon.

A big smile played on Gordon's lips as he gobbled a piece.

I took a huge bite of bacon, letting the taste linger in my mouth, realizing that breakfast with the family was now starting to feel normal.

TWENTY

"The way we look at our children and their limitations is precisely the way they will feel about themselves. We set the examples, and they learn by taking our cue from us."

– Amalia Starr

November 1998

Last month, we were excited when Gordon was able to identify us. But it stopped there. He could only mention our names when asked to identify us in pictures or when pointing to each of us. He would not use our names to get our attention. Labelling and getting one's attention, though they trigger the same response, our names, require different skill sets.

Soon winter would be there. Seasons changed. Our hopes for Gordon to call us by our names did not.

We continued to constantly drill Gordon, and it had become a norm in our family in everything we did. When we walked around the house, we stopped when faced with the wall of pictures. We asked Gordon what color while pointing to a picture of a red train on the wall. If needed, we prompted him to say 'red' or waited until Gordon said it before taking a step farther. We created situations to force him to respond.

At times when we were at McDonald's, we'd present his photo album where he would select among the PECS pictures. He then attached his selection to a sentence strip and gave it to us, so we could order for him. It must have been a relief to express himself, albeit in pictures; he would let out a big chuckle.

Since Gordon loved long rides in the van, we always asked him to tell us who the driver was before he got to experience a joy ride, giving him the opportunity to call us Mom or Dad. I had seen the progress in Gordon's development based on this approach, and working together as a family had brought us closer.

Our friends, aware of our situation, had noticed that we lived, ate, and breathed our home program. The daycare manager and behavior therapist had also jumped on board by using the same approach and lending us toys we could use for our home program.

With the full support of everyone, we were more confident that Gordon would make progress.

Christmas was in the air. Right around the second weekend of November, our favorite radio station aired Christmas tunes to coincide with the Santa Claus Parade marching in downtown Toronto. Bingo brought out the boxes and bins of Christmas decorations.

While waiting for Miguel who would work with Gordon that day, Patrick and I rearranged some furniture by the living room window to clear the way for the Christmas tree which we planned to set up later that afternoon. Gordon circled around the coffee table while babbling at the same time.

"Gordon, stop. Stop walking around," Patrick said, raising his voice to get his attention, but Gordon kept going.

"Mom, how do I get him to stop doing that?" Patrick whined. "It's making me dizzy."

"Tell him."

"But he's not listening to me."

I moved a console table to the corner, then faced Patrick. "What exactly do you want him to do?"

"Stop going around. He's *stimming*, Mom. You said that's not good for him."

"You're telling him what NOT to do, but you're not telling him what to do. Do you get what I mean?" Bingo dropped the last box of Christmas decorations on the floor and stared at me as if I was speaking a foreign language.

Patrick shook his head. "I don't get it."

"Do you want him to just stand there, to go to the basement, or to sit on the sofa? You need to be specific."

"Hmm. Maybe sit down."

"Then tell him that, and if he doesn't do it, guide him to sit on the sofa." I studied his facial expression. "He will stop when you tell him what he is supposed to do."

Patrick guided Gordon to sit on the sofa and handed him the blue Thomas train. "Gordon, sit here, okay?"

Bingo rolled his eyes.

"It's true," I shot back at him. "We cannot assume that Gordon knows the opposite of walking around. When you say, *stop walking around*, then what? Children with autism see black or white. Seeing the in-between, the gray area, requires a higher cognitive level which Gordon is not capable of currently. Just state the positive. The '*negative of*' may not be evident to them."

He shrugged his shoulders, then patted my back, "That's why I married my wife." He seemed resigned at my lengthy explanation and showed little patience to listen to the details.

Shortly after, the doorbell rang. Patrick ran over to the front door to let Miguel in. For the last two months that he'd been with us, we had observed Miguel to be a typical seventeen-year-old high school student who followed current fashion and was an excellent break-dancer at that. *That was good; perhaps he could teach Gordon to dance which would serve as an example of sequence imitation.*

"Whoa," Patrick reacted as he noticed Miguel's orange dyed hair.

"Hey, dude." Miguel gave Patrick a high five.

I escorted Gordon to the foyer to meet Miguel. "C'mon, Gordon, it's time for work. Miguel's here."

In an instant, he slipped out of my grip and ran elsewhere.

"Where did he go? Hey, Gordon, come over here. It's time for work," Miguel yelled out and then acknowledged Bingo's presence. "He's usually eager to work."

Bingo and I just stood there in awe as we watched the quick unfolding of Gordon's disappearance.

"*Flash Gordon*," Bingo said.

With his firm and monotone voice, in the video of their sessions, Gordon seemed to love working with Miguel, in my observation. *Something was off today.*

No words, no explanation, no audible resistance could be heard, but his footsteps as Gordon ran from the kitchen to the living room, in what seemed to be an effort to avoid Miguel today.

Patrick noticed what his brother was doing. "Gordon, come here." Patrick chased after him. "What's up, Gordon? You love working with Miguel, don't you?"

Gordon dragged a kitchen chair and positioned it by the open coat closet. He climbed up the chair, unhooked a baseball cap, and gave it to Miguel.

Miguel glanced at Patrick, wondering why Gordon did that.

Patrick laughed. "Looks like he can't stand the sight of your orange hair."

Miguel chuckled.

We headed to the basement. Despite the strands of Miguel's orange hair peeking through the baseball cap, Gordon cooperated and worked with him as usual.

Bingo followed to the basement but instead of joining us, he opened the door that led to the workroom, then shut it as soon he stepped inside. Housed in that ten-by-ten-foot workroom were Bingo's handyman tools, but it also doubled as a storage room for suitcases and bins of off-season items.

At the end of the session, I entered the workroom to inform Bingo that the session was over. Bingo prepared his hair salon area in the workroom, the only non-carpeted area in the basement. He laid down some newspapers, set out a stool, and brought out the cape. It must have been two years since we'd made the corner of this workroom a hair salon for the boys.

Coincidentally, right after Gordon was diagnosed with autism, he seemed to have developed a sensory issue that getting a haircut became an ordeal. No balloons, lollipops, or popsicles could appease him. He was fuzzy and in tears the whole time. We heeded to our hairdresser's advice in purchasing an electric razor, so Bingo could cut his hair. In having his haircut done at home, Bingo could take his time giving him his buzz cut, and we were not impacting other people's appointments.

Patrick removed his shirt while I removed Gordon's, prepping them for their haircut. Miguel tidied up the program materials as he got ready to leave.

"Who goes first?" I faced Patrick, then flashed a glance at Gordon while pointing to their father.

Gordon, eyes on Patrick, blurted out, "Pepe, eh, eh," while pointing at his brother and then to Bingo.

We all froze, Miguel included, and exchanged glances with one another. *Just like a deaf-mute, he now had gestural communication.*

"Did you hear that, Dad?" Patrick asked.

"What did you say, Gordon?" Miguel bent to Gordon's eye level to have him repeat what we heard.

Gordon let out a hearty laugh and ran over to the other side of the basement, hopped onto the couch, and buried himself in the throw pillows.

I hollered for Rose, about to leave for her weekend off. "Rose, Gordon just called Patrick, 'Pepe.'"

Rose came running down with wide applause.

Bingo rushed over to Gordon. "It's Pepe's turn."

We just witnessed a touchdown, but just like the football game, we could never be sure when the next one would be. In the meantime, I was soaking in the joy I felt inside and couldn't wait to share that with my neighbors, friends, and family.

Pepe was no longer just a label. Gordon had learned it was a name he could use to get his brother's attention. We would soon have our turns. I couldn't wait to hear that sweet sound.

Hallelujah!

TWENTY-ONE

"Why Fit in when you were born to standout?"

– Dr. Seuss

December 1998

Earlier in the year, I signed up for the Geneva Autism Convention held last November in downtown Toronto. I requested Bingo to attend on my behalf when I learned at the last minute that I couldn't take time away from the office because of the heavy workload. After the convention, he briefed me about the presentations and gave me the books and other materials he got, but the highlight of his experience was meeting fellow Filipinos with autistic children.

At the convention, he met Charlie and Fina who invited us to their home that evening. It must have been over two years ago since the last time we attended a social gathering. That was shortly after Gordon had been diagnosed. Back then, his style of playing with objects was odd—anything round, the size of a penny or a plate, was a steering wheel. Anything long and resembling a stick, a pencil or the remote control, was like a baton. He loved to pull wires and cables behind the big TV. I thought that peculiarity was attributed to his terrible-two phase, but when it didn't fade by the time he turned three, and we couldn't divert his attention, we stopped going to other people's homes for fear he might wreck something. When Bingo told me about the invitation, I got excited. We would be with those who were traversing the same road we were.

"We must be here. That's the house," Bingo announced, eyeing the parked cars along the vicinity. Charlie and Fina's house was a two-story single detached brown house with a seventy-five-foot deep front yard.

As we approached the area, the door swung open, the host expecting us.

"Welcome to the autism family," Fina greeted us with a wide smile. I smiled back, noticing that she was quite tall for a Filipino lady. Dressed in slacks and a light silk shirt with a matching cardigan, Fina seemed to have such fine taste in clothes. She took our coats, then escorted us to the living room where the other mothers were seated.

"The children are downstairs in the basement."

After meeting the other mothers, Bingo and the boys headed to the basement while I stayed in the living room.

Everyone was mingling with each other, and I could feel the synergy. Seated with those mothers made me realize how isolated we had been.

"Where do you live?" I approached one of them and felt compelled to ask. She told me she lived in Mississauga. I wondered why I had met none of them, considering they all lived in the next town to Oakville.

"How old is your daughter?" I asked one mom holding on to her girl, who I later learned was the one with autism.

"She's five." She gave her daughter a cookie from the tray.

"Just like Gordon. What does she do now? Does she go to any autism program?" I also helped myself to the butter cookies.

"Yeah. Once a week, she goes to Erin Oaks."

"What's that?" I realized that there were some service providers I was not aware of. She told me more about the agency.

"How did you know about this agency? Who's your doctor?" Either Dr. Pelletier, the diagnosing doctor, was nonchalant about patient care or was not aware of any service providers, which I found hard to believe.

Fina replenished the tray of cookies on the coffee table and sat in the side chair nearest to the sofa.

"How old is Gordon?"

"He turned five two months ago. How about your son?"

"He's nine," she said.

"Is he verbal?"

"He was, early on, then something changed, and he stopped talking."

I didn't know what to say. My jaw dropped. It must have been disheartening to see your son hitting a milestone one day only to realize it was just temporary.

I later learned that she gave birth in her forties and he was the youngest of the four children. We continued to exchange our personal stories.

I reached out to other mothers, learning that every one of them had a story to tell, from the time the autism symptoms manifested to their denial and how their lives had evolved. Our conversation ranged from sharing our personal stories to the services and endowment we were entitled to.

Curious on how the boys were doing, I excused myself to join them in the basement where all the children were gathered.

I saw Patrick with children who appeared to be siblings huddled in a corner. Gordon played with his Matchbox car beside them. Like Gordon, who had no physical deformities, spotting a child with autism was difficult. But a child with autism was always *guarded* by a parent.

"If Gordon does not learn to behave, one of us will always be with him in a social gathering like this," I whispered to Bingo.

The TV was turned on. A child grabbed the remote control, wanting to fast forward the scene. The mother later explained to us that all he wants to see are the credits at the end of the show. Another child kept jumping and flapping his hands, excited at the sight of the show, and there was that child who didn't care about the TV, yet he hummed a low tone while mesmerized at the circling colorful lights in the ceiling. Watching them all together gave me a sense of the breadth of the autism spectrum.

I spotted a father guiding his son on how to run the train in its track. He must have received this new train set this Christmas.

After a quick introduction, I asked, "Is your son verbal?"

The father responded. "Yeah, you know what I mean."

I nodded. The truth was, I didn't know what he meant, and I hoped Gordon would be able to articulate once he reached six years old like his son.

On the way home, I thought of that boy. If he was already *verbal*, what else could their problem be?

Serendipity had to have brought Bingo to meet those families at the convention. The people who are trekking the same journey understood me. I could feel safe sharing my issues and challenges, knowing I wouldn't be judged. *I had found my family.*

TWENTY-TWO

"It's really cool that everybody's a little bit different but the same too"

– Julia: Sesame Street

January 1999

We welcomed the New Year, hoping for new beginnings. Last month, we met with St. Marguerite's school principal, Mr.

McMann, who assured us that Gordon's senior kindergarten teacher, Mrs. Williams, and Educational Assistant (EA), Mrs. Zee, would make it a productive year and keep him safe at all times. Over the Christmas break, we showed Gordon his SK (senior kindergarten) classroom, so he could familiarize himself and feel comfortable that his brother went to the same school, and the daycare was next door. Instead of going to the daycare in the afternoons, he would be attending school. The home program continued with sessions in the morning, late afternoon, and Saturday mornings.

I was happy to note that Gordon adjusted well during the first week. While peering from outside the school grounds, I watched Gordon standing by the monkey bars at the kindergarten yard during their mid-afternoon recess, and I noticed he was surrounded by girls who seemed to be amused with his babbles. They followed his cue, resulting in a chorus of laughter. Shortly after, Gordon twirled—or stimmed—on an object, and they followed his action as well.

Tears welled up in my eyes. His odd behavior of stimming and babbling that I thought would alienate him from his class was making him popular; girls were drawn to him. If only I could read Gordon's mind, the boys' kind of play because the running around did not make sense; it didn't nurture a relationship.

I ha contemplated homeschooling Gordon, but cultivating social development was important as well, and the school environment fostered that.

The school followed the same policy as the day-care wherein we communicated with them using a logbook so any information was always recorded. This logbook also served as our vehicle of communication when I left notes for the teacher and vice versa. At that point, Gordon, by all intentions, was still unable to relay a message and carry a conversation. I left the premises, confident I made the right decision.

***

A week had passed, and a strong winter snow-storm struck our area which resulted in the school and business closure. Our road, considered as tertiary, was not the priority for road plowing and therefore was impassable that morning. We were snowbound; my workers could not make it to our area. While Rose prepared lunch, Bingo and I alternated shoveling our driveway while Patrick and Gordon were downstairs in the basement.

As I tossed the shoveled snow onto a mound, a little boy with curly blond hair peeking out of his red toque, wearing a canary yellow snow jacket, emerged from his hiding place.

I planted my shovel on the mound and approached him. "I'm sorry, did I hit you?"

He shook his head and grinned, exposing a missing tooth.

Without delay, he asked, "Can Gordon come out and play?" His eyes twinkled as he spoke.

"What's your name?" A warm sensation melted my heart. *Gordon had a new friend.*

"Mark," he said in his soft-spoken voice.

"How do you know Gordon?"

"He's in my class."

"How did you get here? Where do you live?" He pointed to a white two-story single detached home about five doors down the street.

I invited him inside.

He looked like a little angel that had descended upon us. I was touched that someone would want to come over and play with my son. What an impression Gordon must have given his class in his first week of school.

"Gordon!" I hollered from the stairway. "There's someone here to see you."

"Who is it, Mom?" Footsteps rushed upstairs from the basement, and Patrick appeared, catching his breath.

I turned to him. "It's Mark, someone from his class. Go get your brother."

Moments later, Patrick got Gordon's snowsuit, toque, gloves, and boots for me to help Gordon bundle up. Once all geared up, they headed straight to the two-meter snowbank and built a tunnel while I watched them from a distance.

"Gordon, this is how you do it." Patrick showed Gordon how to dig with their gloves. Gordon did as Patrick told him. The three of them working together managed to dig a hole big enough for them to crawl through and in and out they went. *Ah, the sweet sound of their hearty laughter.* Their smiles sparkled like the snow surface shimmering against the rays of the sun.

I was over the moon at such a sight that my son had a playmate and thrilled to witness his shining moment. I needed to capture this. *Click, click, click. Those are the photos that told a story.*

***

Gordon seemed to like school because, in the past few weeks, I had witnessed the excitement on his face each time I drove him during the mornings. I knew that Gordon was in good hands, but part of me was still unsettled since Gordon's behavior at school could be unpredictable.

Unlike the chatty kids in his class, Gordon had a guide who helped him express himself. I felt insecure about the situation, knowing Gordon needed to face the *real* world at some point. The first five years of his life revolved around his family, and we knew it was time for him to venture outside his home.

Being a Monday, everyone at work seemed to be quiet and exhausted from the weekend. I reminded myself that Gordon would be all right. *Baby steps.* Scanning my emails, I checked to see which ones I should read first. A buzz intruded, and the telephone's caller ID indicated that someone from the school was calling. *Oh no!* I let it ring at least two times, then took a deep breath and cleared my thoughts before picking up the call. *No one called just to let us know that he was happy and everything was all right.* There was always a reason for the call which gave me chills and took me back to the first call I received from Mrs. Moore of the school's special education department a week ago. I had not met her, but her pleasant voice sounding like whispering meadows calmed me down.

"Mrs. Rivera, we have an issue with Gordon today. He refuses to work and wants to join the kids outside during recess. I just thought I'd let you know that an incident note will be in his school bag today."

My heart stopped. "What happened? Was he detained for recess?"

"Mrs. Zee, his EA, instructed him to stay inside because he refused to finish his work."

"How was he told that he cannot go out for recess?" A loud thud rocked my chest.

"She told him he can only go out to recess after finishing his work."

A light bulb flashed through my mind.

"Mrs. Moore," I slowed down my speech like I was about to lecture my workers during a team meeting. "There is a difference between telling him 'you can go out for recess after finishing your work' versus 'finish your work then you can go out for recess.'"

"Ah."

Presuming her short remark indicated it was still my turn to carry on with the conversation, I continued.

"With Gordon's limited comprehension and span of attention, when you say, 'you can go out for recess after...' his attention stops at 'recess.'" I paused. "Right then and there, he's yearning for that 'reward.' Who doesn't?"

"And?"

"When you say, 'finish your work, then you can go out,' his mind waits for 'what's in it for me,' 'what do I get when I finish my work.' The rule is we need to state the task first then the reward. This rule, by the way, is effective not just for Gordon but anyone, especially those with a limited attention span."

She became silent for a minute, perhaps trying to digest what I just mentioned.

"Oh, I see. Let me share this with Mrs. Williams and Mrs. Zee. Thanks for the tip, Mrs. Rivera."

"Thank you too. I'll write this script in our communication logbook tonight."

"Please do that. Thank you."

I felt good after that call knowing that Mrs. Moore was receptive to my approach and seemed open-minded to other ideas which were a validation that we'd made the right choice for Gordon's placement.

Sometimes, there were 'FYI' calls that didn't stir me up. "Just to let you know that we're going on an ice-skating field trip at the end of the month." I welcomed those calls. They informed us of upcoming activities that Gordon would participate in and helped us prepare him for that activity.

Then there were calls that were unsettling, like that of today.

I clung to the receiver, dreading the call.

"Mrs. Rivera, this is Mrs. Moore. The reason for this call is that I need to inform you we noticed Gordon has been entering our kindergarten yard before the bell rings."

I transferred the phone to my left ear. "Is there a problem with that?"

"Yes, because we don't have an EA to supervise him during that time, and we ask that your nanny bring Gordon to school exactly at one p.m. and not before that."

I was sensing the purpose of that call, and I was not sure I liked what I heard. "I'm sorry?"

"I mean, we can't have him in the kindergarten yard before…"

"No, I am not taking this." I cut her off.

"He can wait in the parking area with your nanny before one p.m."

Despite the effort in trying to maintain my composure, I could no longer mask the tension bubbling inside me. "First of all, you know very well that my son is fascinated with cars. If he waits in the parking area, I can guarantee you that he will be inspecting the cars and vans. We are talking about a safety issue, and if something happens to him, I will have to hold you accountable for that," I gasped.

"Secondly, can you please reinstate the scope of your inclusion policy? Does it specify that my son is included in all the activities the other children are participating *with an exception of*?"

I took a deep breath and didn't leave room for her to speak. My heart rate felt like I went through an intense workout, and my calm, indoor voice had just flown out the window; my coworkers could now hear me.

"Thirdly, you are aware that I have a nanny whom I pay to keep an eye on my son. I have not requested for your EA to supervise him during this time, have I?"

"Er...ah..." she stammered.

"I'm sorry. I can't take this." I hung up.

Drying my tears, I couldn't believe what I just heard.

Just when I had thought everything was going smoothly, I had hit a snag.

TWENTY-THREE

"Autism . . . offers a chance for us to glimpse an awe-filled vision of the world that might otherwise pass us by."

– Dr. Colin Zimbleman, Ph.D.

June 1999

Bingo and I, together with the Gordon's school team—Mr. McMann, the principal; Mrs. Moore, the special education itinerant; Mrs. Williams, Mrs. Zee; and others from the school board's special education department—were gathered at the school's conference room to discuss Gordon's education plan and placement for next school year.

We were first presented with Gordon's strengths and development needs as had been observed in the school setting. On the agenda item on placement, Bingo and I requested that Gordon be retained in SK since he was not on par with his classmates in academic and social development skills. He didn't raise his hands as his classmates did. I wondered if he knew his classmates' names or if he did, did he call them by their name?

"Mr. and Mrs. Rivera, just to let you know, Mrs. Williams and Mrs. Zee will also be moving up to grade one next year. Mrs. Williams will be teaching Gordon's class and Mrs. Zee will continue to be his EA."

"Really?" Bingo's eyes opened wide.

I jolted back. We were both in disbelief, yet at the same time, touched by that news. I wondered if their move was meant for Gordon or had it always been in the plan. Whatever the intent was, their decision showed the school's commitment to partnering with us for Gordon's welfare.

"But..." I imagined how overwhelming the grade one curriculum would be for him. My voice cracked. "He can't even articulate *Patrick*; he calls him *Pepe* instead." My insecurity crept in.

"We are aware of that. One more thing," Mr. McMann added. "We will also make sure that his core group, the children who hang out with him, will be in his same class in grade one."

I froze, gaping at him, then let out a smile. That news had unexpectedly taken me aback. "That's awesome."

I saw compassion in Mrs. Moore's eyes. "He'll get there, Mrs. Rivera," she assured us.

Although I was not convinced by her reassurance, I realized that we couldn't predict the future.

She continued. "Gordon has made some improvements since he started school."

Improvements? Maybe Gordon had made a lot of improvements which I never noticed. Friends and neighbors had also shared the same comments.

My thoughts shifted to last month to Mother's Day. Bingo roused him from his bed and handed Gordon the card he made in school, so he could give it to me. With Bingo's fingers pointing to the words, Gordon said, 'Happy Mama Day."

"What? Can you say that again?" I covered my face as the mist filled my eyes.

Patrick came running after I hollered. I embraced Gordon so tight and didn't want to let go and just savored that moment. Patrick and Bingo embraced me, and we all shared a group hug.

What a wonderful feeling to be called Mama, especially on that day. Despite a nippy spring day, I opened the windows and raised my voice. "I am a Mama." The fragrance of the lilacs could not be ignored, and if I could hear the symphony, the flowers also greeted me, saying, "Happy Mama Day."

Mr. McMann stroked his peppery beard. He nodded at me, bringing my attention back to the purpose of the meeting.

"I don't see Gordon all the time, but they both do." He gestured to Mrs. Williams and Mrs. Zee who sat across from him. "But I have observed great improvements in him. He has made a lot of strides."

I nodded to acknowledge his observation. Hearing those words reminded me to be more cognizant of the positive changes in Gordon's behavior since we had started our home program and he had started school. I looked up at them with misty eyes. "I agree. He's a changed boy now—a happier boy. He is much more aware of his surroundings." I looked at each and every one of them surrounding the rectangular table. "We have to give all of you a lot of credit for that. Thank you."

Bingo squeezed my hand like he appreciated the compliments I gave them on his behalf.

I faced Mrs. Moore. "In the event Gordon experiences pressure, can we set him back to SK?"

"We will discuss that when you get there."

"That sounds fair." I concurred. I decided we would have to give the school system a chance.

On our way home after the meeting, Bingo asked me what I thought of Gordon's grade one placement in the fall. Since he and I were raised in a school system that held back a child not qualified to be moved up, we shared the same view. We were insecure if it was the right move for Gordon, but we were not offered an alternative. I knew that when I was faced with no option, the challenges enabled me to reach for the stars and realize my potential. *Maybe we should not make life too easy for him. Perhaps that would be for the best.*

"I guess we have a lot of catch-up work to do between now and then," I said, resigned at that thought.

***

October 1999

Setting aside my emotions regarding Gordon's placement for the upcoming school year, I zeroed in my research on strategies to teaching conversation. I happened to visit our community library where I saw children and parents signing out some books-on-tape. I grabbed a few based on the *Arthur* television series, the only series they have available where the tapes are accompanied with books.

When I got home, I experimented with my new idea on Gordon. In the living room, away from the TV, I attached the headset on him and opened the book. While the cassette player was narrating the story, I pointed my fingers to the words of the book. I stepped back and observed him 'reading' on his own. To my surprise, Gordon did not demonstrate any aggression and seemed to show interest in the experiment, *and maybe the story too.*

After one book, I asked, "Are you up for another book?"

Although he didn't respond, I put in another cassette and grabbed the next book. He 'read' another book-on-tape from the same series while I headed to the kitchen to grab myself a cup of tea. I watched him from afar. *I wondered if the animated narration and catchy intonation held his interest much better than when I read books to him.* I smiled to myself like I had uncovered something.

Bingo appeared by the hallway and studied us. "Is that damaging to him?"

"I hope not." I glanced at him. "We need to do as much as we can because he will be grade one in the fall. At least his hands are not stimming on something when he's reading." He gave me a thumbs-up.

Since the books-on-tape were not available at the store, I continued to renew our subscription at the library, so Gordon wouldn't lose momentum.

After Gordon finished reading the two books, Bingo got him ready with his soccer gear. He called on Patrick so the two of them could train Gordon how to play soccer in our backyard. Bingo had signed him up for soccer with children two years younger than him.

While I prepared Gordon to be school-ready, Bingo prepared him to be in the sports department. An extracurricular activity, like sports, also fostered one's social development. I was fortunate that I could count on Bingo for sports activities.

***

In addition to the *Arthur* books-on-tape, we had noticed his interest in the *Arthur* TV show as well. To augment his interest, we had also plastered our walls with *Arthur* visuals. Materials for the home program were also based on the *Arthur* TV series. That compelled me to throw an *Arthur*-themed party.

Bantings, banners, and a 'Happy birthday, Gordon' streamer decked the party room of Hopedale

Bowling Lanes. I scanned the corner table filled with loot bags to see if there were enough for each kid, then checked the two long tables adjoined if it could fit sixteen children, then sighed in relief. It was going to be an awesome birthday party, and each of them would also be able to bring home the balloon which was tied to each chair.

After two games of bowling, nine girls and four boys gathered around Gordon, their eyes fixed on the dancing flames of the six candles planted on his birthday cake while cheering him on to blow, as if they were about to witness a momentous once-in-a-lifetime event.

If those children could lift Gordon up to the pedestal, I was sure they would. I felt my goosebumps at the sight of them giving him all their attention and cheering him on in full force. I recalled Mr. McMann's promise in our last meeting that his friends would be in the same class. What a wonderful birthday present!

"Blow, blow." Their enthusiasm was so contagious that Gordon imitated their act and snuffed the flames all at once.

"Yeah, Gordon." They cheered and clapped in delight.

Gordon glanced at them, then let out a big laugh. The children echoed his laughter which triggered everyone to join in the fun.

Indeed, it was a momentous occasion. While those children may have blown their candles on their own on their second birthday, they didn't realize that they had just witnessed Gordon's *first* on his sixth birthday, a milestone that would forever be etched in our memory.

TWENTY-FOUR

"Reach for the sky!"
– Woody, Toy Story

September 2000

Since the start of our Home Program two years ago, the focus had centered on promoting his imitation skills which I have learned was the foundation of natural learning. I was thrilled to learn after reading Gordon's report card that not only was he popular with his classmates, but imitation skills had become one of his strengths. Since we were teaching him to ask questions in our home program and imitate his classmates, Gordon now applied that *asking* skill to his classmates and teachers.

At school, Patrick introduced Gordon to his friend. In response, Gordon asked the friend, "Where do you live?" followed by "When is your garbage collection?" While some children got tickled with those questions and replied with a chuckle, the adults, especially the teachers, were not comfortable responding. My attention was called to coach Gordon the proper timing of when to ask certain questions.

No sooner, he shifted to asking, "Where do you go to church?" If someone didn't go to church, he insisted, "Where?"

Just when he had learned to ask questions, he was now forbidden to ask certain questions. But how do you teach a child with limited comprehension when to ask and when not to ask? Is there a list of *certain* questions? How do you help him visualize that in between black and white, there is gray?

After Christmas break, Gordon was eager to get back to school, but his excitement wore off before the end of February. For no reason, he started pulling down all the posters. "No blue today," he declared. Before he could be responsible for more damage, Mrs. Zee got him out of the scene and brought him to the library.

In another incident toward the end of that month, the children were lined up as usual in the hallway. Sunrays were streaming into the classroom as if to welcome the children back after the noon recess playing in the snow. Just when they were about to march inside, Gordon, who always insisted on being at the head of the line, was like a man on a mission. He stormed inside, rearranged the tables and chairs, and tossed the children's backpacks aside.

Acting on her instincts, Mrs. Williams stretched her arms across the entrance to block the children from entering the classroom. "Gordon, no!" she yelled to stop him. With his mouth shut tight, Gordon paid no attention, focused his eyes on his target objects, and carried on with his task. Confused, some children raised their eyebrows while others covered their mouths. All looked puzzled and horrified to make the attempt to go near him or take a step inside the classroom. That time I got a call from Mrs. Moore who painted the scene for me and requested me to pick up Gordon and take him home. I let out a heavy breath at the news and shifted my focus from my work to the purpose of the call. My heart was ripped apart. Listening to her, I slumped into my office chair and found myself gazing at the paper clutter on top of my desk. The sight of the clutter probably resembled the chaos in the classroom right now. I thought of those children, Gordon's circle of friends, who couldn't fathom what their golden boy was capable of. I was embarrassed that they were witnessing that ugly side of Gordon. I contemplated pulling him out.

Mrs. Moore and I discussed the situation and weighed our options. Coming across in her soft-spoken and diplomatic tone, she helped me assess the situation with some levelheadedness. Then I deliberated. "Is pulling him out a positive reinforcement that propagates the act or negative reinforcement?" I paused to listen to her "hmm" seemingly acknowledging what I was saying. "I am afraid that if we pull him out now, he'll do the same act tomorrow to be pulled out again. Children cheer for 'no school,' don't they? What do you think?"

After thinking it through, Mrs. Moore concurred with my assessment and agreed to let him stay in school and be redirected in the meantime. "Can we meet next week to discuss these behaviors?"

I had been charting Gordon's aggressive behavior in the hopes of seeing some patterns. During the meeting with Mrs. Moore and Mrs. Williams, among those in attendance, I shared with them my functional analyses of Gordon's behavior.

"Some behaviors could be attention seeking." I glanced at those in attendance.

"I can see that," Mrs. Williams said. "One time, he purposely spelled the word wrong but before he could finish to correct himself, he looked around to see if all eyes were on him. He loves his classmates' reaction." We all laughed. "He has a great sense of humor; I have to admit," she added.

"Some could be avoidance, especially when tasks at hand prove to be quite overwhelming for him. When we started the home program, he was overturning the tables and chairs. But as he learned, those behaviors started to go away." They nodded, perhaps in agreement. They must have been thinking of similar examples in their experiences with him.

"What about these past aggressive behaviors?" Mrs. Moore seemed anxious about what precipitated the calling of this meeting.

Bingo offered his view. "That is sad." We all looked at Bingo who just made his presence known now, thirty minutes into the meeting. He continued. "I mean SAD–seasonal affective disorder."

When lost, my tendency was to read up on any related literature while Bingo consulted families in our support group and other friends. SAD, or the lack of sunlight, we understood could affect anyone, not only those with a diagnosis. Some people's behavior could not be explained as they fought their depression which was triggered by the lack of sunlight.

"I think we need to be cognizant that Gordon could be affected by the lack of sunlight. Unfortunately, since he is not able to articulate his emotions, he resorts to some aggressive behavior," I suggested to Mrs. Moore and Mrs. Williams. From then on, SAD around February was noted on Gordon's school records.

True enough, by spring, just when the leaves were coming back, when the migratory birds were back from the south, Gordon was back, the golden boy with a sense of humor. We had more sunlight during this time, and in fact, by June, the sun set close to ten in the evening.

That summer, we drove to Disney World. Looking up to Mickey Mouse and Minnie Mouse, Gordon was captivated that those characters we'd been talking about in his home program were real.

During the long drive from Toronto to Orlando and back, he did not bat an eyelash for fear he would miss something. By the time we got home, he blurted out, "So, 'Speed Limit' in the US and 'Maximum' in Canada?"

From being nonverbal to asking that keen sense of observation, I had to conclude that my son had developed so much in grade one.

***

November 2001

Gordon was now in grade two. Mr. McMann had retired, and Mrs. Hanes had taken over as the principal. In lieu of Mrs. Williams and Mrs. Zee, Mrs. Ramos and Mrs. White were Gordon's teacher and EA respectively in the new grade.

After dinner, I observed Gordon heeding to Patrick's orders as they put away the dishes. Gordon loved imitating Patrick. It was like a game. Attributing to a structured schedule since we embarked on the home program, it was noted now that he followed a routine quite well. With all the labels plastered throughout our walls, the report card also noted his good retention in high-frequency sight words.

The sight of the two of them interacting made my heart leap with joy. I hoped that they would continue to have the need for each other in their adulthood.

"What are you smiling about?" Bingo caught me grinning while in a daze.

"Just listen to your boys." I gestured toward their direction.

"Gordon, put plate here," Patrick said. Like a good soldier, Gordon heeded to his brother's orders. A hearty laugh from both of them ensued.

I faced Bingo. "I can now see what other people have been telling us. He's come a long way in the past two years."

"Yeah," Bingo said dryly, with no intent to savor the moment with me. Then he tossed the black communication logbook. "Have you read today's report?"

Hmmph. Oh no. That sounded like some undesirable behavior could have happened at school. But why couldn't he enjoy that moment with me? "Good or bad?" I twitched my lips and rolled my eyes. With that tone, I was not sure I was eager to read that report.

"Just read it."

"Gordon refused to work during math class today. He threw the spinning wheel we used to illustrate the probability of hitting the color quadrant," I read the report aloud.

My mood shifted. I glanced back at my happy boys then at Bingo. "What do you want me to say?" I was usually quick in sharing my thoughts, but often these days, I wanted to factor in his thoughts as well. I liked to hear his perspective too.

"I expected that," he said.

"Whoa, whoa, wait a minute. What do you mean?" I had to ask. More than ten years married to Bingo, and I hadn't learned to read his mind. He shot back a conclusion without any warning.

"He can't even watch *Wheel of Fortune*," he blurted out.

I was quiet for a moment as I allowed my thoughts to roll back to the time prior to Gordon's diagnosis when he was mesmerized with spinning objects. We had stopped using our ceiling fans as he tended to stare at one for as long as it spun.

I opened my eyes wide. "Haven't you noticed that Gordon doesn't spin those round objects anymore? He doesn't *stim* with them?"

I expected him to be ecstatic with this positive change but a nod from him was all I got. "C'mon, Bingo. Look at the positive side. Be happy. As everyone has said, he has made so much progress."

"Okay." He shrugged. "Let us suggest to them to draw lots from a brown paper bag instead. It is also as effective as spinning the wheel to illustrate probability."

"Love that idea. That's a good one. I know I can count on you for brilliant ideas." My eyes sparked at that thought. I easily got annoyed with his abrupt conclusion, but I was in awe when he came up with such ideas. "Remember when we talked about the functional analysis of a behavior?" I waited to see his attention was on me. "This aggressive behavior could be attributed to a sensory issue, the stomach pangs. He may be getting some stomach pangs at the sight of that spinning wheel."

"There you go." He gave me a thumbs-up.

As I wrote the explanation into the communication logbook, I wondered why I did not receive a call for this incident, like his previous outbursts.

Just as I finished writing in the communication logbook, Gordon, with Patrick behind him, came to me, bringing the Candyland board game. "Play game?" he asked.

We had introduced that game in our home program to teach turn-taking, and because the game did not require any reading, it had easily become Gordon's favorite.

"Sure, Gordon dear. Just say it, and we'll play Candyland." I glanced at Bingo then at the boys, recalling when Gordon had no desire to involve us in his world. Our life had been like Candyland. We stepped through many colors before we could have the taste of the coveted life in the candy castle.

TWENTY-FIVE

"Our duty in autism is not to cure but to relieve suffering and to maximize each person's potential."

– John Elder Robison

September 2006

Our home program stopped after Gordon completed grade two. We released our live-in nanny, Rose, from her employment with us. Without a caregiver over the last five years, we have sent the boys to a sitter for their before and after-school care.

Rose left us with a valuable collection of VHS tapes of the home program she had recorded. Labeled in her penmanship, I often thought of her as she had moved on to another employer. Heaven sent Rose into our lives when we needed her most. The dining room that had been used as her work area for creating labels and other materials for the home program had now been reclaimed for its real function.

We started a tradition of having our Sunday candlelight dinner with the background music of Patrick's selection. The meals always began with a prayer of thanks not only for the food but for the blessings we had received. Gordon got a kick out of it to include the sunny day, *Lolo* and *Lola* (referring to his grandfather and grandmother), our family, and anything else he could think of, among our blessings, which triggered a good laugh before we dug in. Bingo would tap my forearm to turn my attention to our two boys sharing school stories. The current ambiance made me realize that we could now let go of the stressors and turbulent times, knowing we could have some pleasant evenings as a family.

We just got back from our summer vacation in the Philippines, our first time since we started the home program. While Bingo spent most of his time in the northern part of the Philippines where he was originally from, I stayed in the southern part, with the boys splitting their time between both areas.

I was in the master bedroom unpacking our clothes from the trip.

"Pat." I handed him the stack of clothes. "Can you put this back in the closet?" I examined the room. "By the way, where's your brother?"

"Sshh," Patrick replied with his forefinger on his lips. "He's in his room, reading."

I approached Gordon's bedroom and noticed that his door was open. Not wanting to intrude, I admired him from a distance, proud that he was delighted about reading during his pastime.

I hadn't stopped sharing the good news with my friends and family. From reading frequently sighted words in grade one to learning to read words phonetically in grade two. But he had never caught the bug for reading. I often wondered if the interest in reading was teachable. My personal belief was having the bug for reading came from one's interest, either innate or one's exposure to the subject matter. A child interested in sports and not in sci-fi topics could not be forced to read sci-fi books.

My thoughts rewound back to last spring when Gordon broached the idea of taking Kumon classes. It was very unlike Gordon to ask for something. He had never requested an edible treat, a toy, or a place to go. But when he needed help in learning, we never denied his request. I wondered if he felt behind compared to his classmates. Having that sense would be a testament to his awareness of his surroundings.

Bingo and I were both supportive of his request. Ever since we ceased our home program, there'd been a void in our life which no longer contained structure. Gone was our need to rush home and stay up late at night to review Gordon's progress. We also missed our workers who had helped us along the way.

On our way to the closest Kumon center, Gordon blurted out, "Not here, please go to Maple Grove." I always got annoyed when he insisted on his direction that didn't make sense. His preferred center was not the closest Kumon location, but I acquiesced to his wishes to avoid an argument for fear that he would decide not to proceed with Kumon.

This Kumon center operated twice a week in the hall of a church. Upon arrival, we saw children of grade school age working on their worksheets.

Mrs. Gonzales, the administrator, stood tall, dressed in a blouse with a four-inch sash that accentuated her waist and a matching skirt. "You must be Gordon." With her Hispanic accent, she extended her hand to Gordon. "Welcome."

After addressing Gordon, she faced me. "Good afternoon, Mrs. Rivera. Come this way." Mrs. Gonzales led us to a long table where she had her 'office' set up. Gordon and I sat across from each other.

To break the ice, she asked Gordon, "What school do you go to, Gordon?"

I noticed Gordon was tight-lipped with no intention to respond to her question. He looked toward the other direction like he was watching a movie scene of children doing their homework.

I eyed her until she caught my gaze. I made signs for us to step outside, then to Gordon, I said, "Stay here. We'll be right back."

Out of Gordon's earshot, I explained to her about his situation. "My son has autism. I don't think you would notice that when he's quiet, but believe me, he has his ways. This is his own initiative to take Kumon," I emphasized. "He has requested for this several times. Please don't ask about school or anything. He wants no one to know that he's taking Kumon. Consider this his secret."

"Oh, I see." Her eyes twinkled with a touch of mischief. She offered a wide grin.

"Thanks for being such a good sport." We headed back to her office.

"Gordon, here are your pamphlets for the week which are the required readings and questions you need to answer. You'll need to submit this to me by next week." She offered a bemused smile.

Gordon nodded. Expressionless and motionless, he looked like he was guarding his personal space.

"Next week when you return, you will work on a worksheet at the center like the other kids."

Gordon kept nodding to her instructions as if saying, *I got it. Yes, to everything you are saying and about to say.* He was just being respectful, but I could see he had no patience for these instructions.

Since then, he'd been working on his Kumon worksheet. I checked his work and helped him whenever he encountered any difficulty. He also brought some worksheets for our trip, and I made sure that he completed all of them.

Patrick's tap on my shoulder brought me back to the present time. "Where do you want me to put these?" he asked.

"Aren't you proud of your brother?" Then I replied to his question. "In the closet. Pat, can you read while lying down on your tummy?" I pointed to Gordon who did that.

"No," he says with little thought. "That's very uncomfortable. I can only last a minute doing that."

I'd always thought that reading position was the most uncomfortable. Gordon was just like my brother Vittorio with whom he shared his fascination for cars, airplanes, and now this reading position. They were the only two people in the world I knew who could read this way.

It takes one to know one, so they say. Their similarities were further confirmed on a trip when Patrick at sixteen years old and Gordon at twelve years old flew as unaccompanied minors on a domestic flight within the Philippines. At their arrival, my brother, Vittorio asked them about their flight experience.

The hour-and-a-half flight experience put a smile on Gordon's face that could not be ignored. It was a treat that he would never forget.

"The seats are this wide." With a wide smile, Gordon positioned his hands at his sides as he demonstrated the roomy seats in business class accommodation. "They said, 'Mr. Rivera' to me." He was tickled being addressed formally. In contrast to Patrick, who had no reaction because for him, all flight accommodations were the same.

It seemed Vittorio had piqued Gordon's interest in flight. From then on, Gordon had started his inflight magazine collections.

As we continued unpacking, the telephone rang. After the call, I turned to Patrick. "That was Mrs. Lee." I was referring to his piano teacher. "You'll resume your lessons on September 21st."

"How about me? When will I have lessons?" Gordon overheard me from his bedroom. With heavy footsteps, he came rushing to my bedroom.

Patrick and I exchanged glances. Patrick used to take piano lessons with a student teacher in the neighborhood. After achieving his grade eight certification, his teacher didn't feel qualified to teach Patrick for the higher grades. She referred us to Mrs. Lee, a seasoned teacher and an adjudicator in the music festivals that he had been competing in and with whom he had been taking lessons for two years now. Each time I drove Patrick for his lessons, Gordon would come and stay quiet the whole time. He had never shown an interest in piano.

"I wonder if he has been observing Mrs. Lee," Patrick whispered to me.

I shrugged, then faced Gordon. "I didn't know you want to take piano lessons."

"Of course, I do." With an unwavering response, I knew nothing could make him change his mind.

"How about having Patrick give you lessons?" I suggested since Patrick was taking students for piano lessons.

"Nope," came his curt reply.

"Let's look for a teacher in the area. That way, we don't have to make a trip to Mississauga."

"No, thank you." His response sounded like he had a promising future as a concert pianist. As a frustrated pianist myself, I felt the warmth radiating in my body. What-if thoughts scattered in my head.

I made a phone call to Mrs. Lee about Gordon's desire to have lessons with her.

She reasoned out, "But, Leah, I don't have experience with special needs children."

"You have to take him, please."

"Mom," Patrick called for my attention. I covered the mouthpiece as I turned to him. "Tell her Gordon has a good sense of rhythm," Patrick whispered as he wrinkled his eyebrows and seemed convinced that we had the making of a professional. We could hardly contain our elation, but Gordon just sat at the edge of the bed, calm as usual, but with a determined look that he takes his lessons with Mrs. Lee and no other person.

I relayed that to Mrs. Lee. And she said, "My schedule is full right now. If I have a spot in mid-afternoon, can you make it?"

"Yes, we will," I cheered in delight, excited that Gordon would be taking piano lessons like his brother. I would have to take time off one afternoon a week, I thought. Anything for my boy.

***

Life was good. The school staff had witnessed a remarkable change in Gordon too. They loved his sense of humor and his pleasant personality.

At the start of the school year, we were informed that Gordon would be sharing an EA with another child. Unsure if that move was in Gordon's best interest, I reminded them that whatever happens, not to call me when Gordon started acting up or being disruptive. The teacher would have to carry on with the lessons for the rest of the class."

As soon as we arrived home in the afternoons, Gordon did his Kumon worksheet in the kitchen while I prepared dinner. After dinner in the evenings, I helped him with schoolwork and piano.

By November, a month after he turned thirteen, I read reports of his noncompliance to assigned tasks in school in the communication logbook. *But it wasn't even February yet.* My mind raced in search of answers. I feared this noncompliance would escalate to class disruption in February.

Despite being regarded as a minor incident, I was compelled to address his noncompliance. At home, I reminded him, "You have to comply with everything they ask you to do in school. Please do it their way."

Another instance to illustrate to him about the authority's word rules was when I guided him for his piano practice at home. I asked him to play the piece three times, for example.

"Only two times," he insisted.

"Who am I?" I asked.

"Mom."

"No, I am the teacher," I said firmly and repeated the question. "Who am I?"

"Teacher."

"Yes, and whatever the teacher says, you do it, ok?"

"Yes, Teacher."

"Okay, let's play this, five times."

I had to detach myself and be the teacher when I was guiding him, but mommy role resumed after the lesson.

Gordon wrote an apology letter for the noncompliance incident. I usually wrote the letter as he narrated to me what happened. The letter always ends with 'and if this promise I should break or if I bring you sorrow, then help me to begin again and keep my promise tomorrow,' which was also the last statement of their school prayer. He then copied what I had written so he could read it to the teacher or to whoever he had offended.

Toward the end of the school year, the incidents had become disruptive and rampant. At home, we noticed that he often growled for no reason. We believed it was an attention-seeking behavior, so we didn't give in to his demands. But when Gordon felt ignored, his growls grew louder, and he started throwing objects.

"We have noticed the changes in his voice." I shared the new experience of random outbursts with a mother in our support group during one of our gatherings.

"How old is Gordon?" she asked as she narrowed her eyes.

"Twelve."

She shook her head and suggested, "They could be attributed to puberty." Then, she added, "He's confused. He cannot comprehend the changes he's going through."

My chest tightened, and my thoughts ran rampant as I asked the men around. Most attested to the *awful* feeling they went through during this phase.

I glanced at Bingo, hoping he could share some comforting words. He shrugged his shoulders.

We were now navigating uncharted waters. All throughout life, there would always be uncharted waters.

TWENTY-SIX

"The most interesting people you'll find are ones
that don't fit into your average cardboard box.
They'll make what they need, they'll make their
own boxes."

– Dr. Temple Grandin

April 2009

Once confined in his own world focused on his repetitive play, Gordon, at fifteen years old, had widened his interests and horizon. He had grown to enjoy reality TV shows, *American Idol*, *Survivor*, *Amazing Race*, *The Voice*, *America's Got Talent*, among others. His interest started when Clay Aiken, an autism/ABA advocate, vied for the *American*

Idol title. He was also a fan of Ellen DeGeneres. What a treat it was for him when we toured Hollywood last summer, and he had his picture taken at the grand staircase of the Kodak Theatre, the site of the *American Idol* finale. Each time he expressed his interests, we were proud of him for those thrilling moments that added a pulse to our hearts.

There were also instances when our heartbeats pounded faster for a different reason, when outbursts occurred. Like any parent, we dreamed that Gordon would acquire academic skills just like everyone else, but his depth of understanding was difficult to assess. That was where we needed to choose our battles. His autism behavior issues stood in the way of his learning. Since the latter part of his elementary years, other than core subjects, his IEP (individualized education plan) had allowed him to choose a subject of interest. Now in high school, we saw no need for him to take chemistry, for example. I doubted he would ever see the practical application for that subject in real life. We helped him choose what interested him.

He still loved to ask people for their church preference. After taking world religion class, Gordon was now aware of diversities: some people practiced different faiths, went to different places of worship, and some didn't practice at all. Still, it had not wavered his faith. It had not also changed how he related to others of different faiths.

We were thrilled that he spoke with spontaneity, a far cry from the prediction he either be nonverbal or would speak in a robotic manner. To strangers who doubted his real diagnosis judging from his manner of speaking, we simply replied, "Stay with us for twenty-four hours, and you'll see." That was the good and the unfortunate thing about autism, they looked perfectly normal, but there was something in them.

We were also ecstatic that he used his speech to express his wants.

One evening, after a year in high school, Gordon approached me in the master bedroom where I was threading a needle to replace a button on my blouse.

Out of the blue, Gordon asked, "Can I take the city bus to school?" His high school was five kilometers away. As a special needs student, he was picked up and dropped off at our doorstep. *Why take the city bus?* I wondered.

Unsure if I heard him correctly, I set my work aside and faced him. "You mean, the Oakville Transit?"

"Yes, bus twenty." Confident in his response, but in a somber tone, he sounded like he had done his research for this well thought-out plan, but his facial expression and voice intonation did not reveal any tinge of excitement.

Map study had been his favorite pastime these days. His collection consisted of the map of the world, Canada, United States, the Philippines, transit maps, and mall maps. We dared not challenge his sense of direction. I was constantly reminded of my prayers shortly after he got diagnosed, and again after seeing the movie *Mercury Rising* where it featured a non-verbal boy with autism who had a keen sense of direction. *God, if it is your will that he remains non-verbal, please bless him a sense of direction so he could find his way home when lost.*

We noticed his interest in the public transit system when Rose, our nanny, came to visit us a few years ago. Knowing Gordon's fascination for cars, she had planned to treat him to a spin in her new car to the mall. But as soon as they got out of the house, he was not interested in her car. He insisted that they take the public bus. As Rose explained to us, he scanned the map at every bus shelter. By the time, they got to the mall, he approached the concierge for a mall map. He studied the map, looked around and associated the shops from his vantage point to their location on the map. After his mall orientation, he asked Rose that they got back home. Oh, the big smile on his face and the walk that looked like he was floating on air upon their arrival. What a treat it was! Though not one she planned for, Rose's eyes sparkled, happy knowing that Gordon enjoyed the afternoon.

"Mom?" Gordon called out to me.

I shook my head and blinked a few times, trying to process his request.

"Uhh," I stuttered. "Let me think about it. Just stay there. Let me clear this with Dad." I preferred a unanimous decision.

Downstairs in the family room, Bingo was sprawled on the couch. I gave him a recap of Gordon's request.

"Seriously? He wants to take the city bus?" As surprised as I was, he arched his eyebrows and sat up straight.

"That's what he said, and with confidence at that," I confirmed, a frown on my face.

"Let him take the city bus. He'll be okay." He gave his approval without giving it much thought.

"Huh?" I cocked my head to the right, surprised at Bingo's approval. "What if he'll have outbursts in public?" I argued. "Do you remember what happened at the after-school child care program?"

The chilling memory of that day still haunted me.

Right when the afternoon snacks of juice and cookies were brought to the center, Gordon ambushed the attendant and knocked down the tray.

"Oh no!" the children screamed. Clearly shaken at what just happened, the children cringed with their arms around themselves, staring at the snacks splattered all over the ground.

After repeated similar events like that, Gordon was expelled from the program.

"But school ends in five weeks. Can he stay until then?" I choked and begged, but my efforts were not enough to make them change their minds. Fortunately, our neighbor across the street was willing to look after Gordon at my house.

"That was two years ago." Sarcastically, he downplayed my example. *Either I was such an overbearing mother, or he was just unconcerned.*

Sensing my trepidation, Bingo added, "When Gordon was young, he wouldn't verbalize his wants. Now he's asking permission. The only way to find out is to have him do it, right?"

I could tell Bingo was also torn. We were cognizant that the disruptive behavior was attributable to his puberty stage, but we hadn't discussed it or sought help on how to mitigate that behavior. All we were doing right now was guarding him close, but we couldn't avoid the damages that could happen when he was out there on his own. Hmm. That was such a big struggle for us since we'd always wished for him to be normal like everyone else.

Back in the master bedroom, Gordon hadn't changed his position since I left him. With a slumped posture, he fiddled with his fingers while waiting for my decision.

"Do you really want to do this?" I wanted him to sense my reluctance.

"Yes," he muttered.

Hoping to dissuade him, I explained the implications of taking the city bus. "First of all, the school bus picks you up at our doorstep and takes you to school. You don't need to walk. If you take the city bus, you walk fifteen minutes to the bus stop, and when you get off, that will be another fifteen minutes of walking to school. Think about how that feels during the winter." I glanced at him, searching for signs if he sensed my concerns.

He shrugged.

I carried on without waiting for a verbal response from him. "Second to that matter, the school bus arrives at seven thirty in the morning. You will need to start walking at six fifty in the morning to catch the city bus that leaves at seven-oh-five, which means you have to wake up early." Unsure if I was making a strong point from his perspective, I added, "Third, the school bus is free, while the city bus is not. Given that, you must bring your wallet at all times."

Silence crossed between us. He raised his eyebrows as if saying, "So, what?" It dawned on me that those implications could be lame excuses after all since he'd been taking the city bus with Patrick for the past three summers to attend their summer programs. He was aware of the schedule, the walk to and from the bus stop, and the responsibility of carrying a wallet.

I took a deep breath to deliver my real reservation for letting him take the city bus. I moved closer and cupped his two hands in mine. "I worry about your safety out there and not to mention your tantrums. I worry about the strangers who may not understand you or may hurt you." I nodded a few times while staring at him. *"I am worried."*

Ever since his diagnosis, we had been open with Gordon about his condition. I wanted to be upfront with him about our concerns as well.

Bingo joined us in the master bedroom and negotiated with Gordon. "Let's do this gradually. Are you okay with taking the city bus on Fridays only?"

"Yes." His nod came quick, right before Bingo finished the question.

Bingo and Gordon huddled over the transit map as Bingo, acting like a general giving last-minute instructions to his unit before they head to the battlefield, interrogated Gordon on the transit routes and schedule. "What if this bus will be late, what will you do?" Gordon responded with confidence. Bingo and I exchanged glances. No doubt, Gordon had studied all of this. In Bingo's assessment, he passed with flying colors. As I watched how things unfolded, I was filled with optimism, knowing his capability of researching and expressing himself when he wanted something.

We informed the school staff of his Friday schedule. The next few days, I sensed an empty feeling in the pit of my stomach during the time he was in transit. I didn't do anything but pray for his safety and stare at the phone for two hours. No phone call meant good news. I closed my eyes and released a sigh. Thank God!

While joy surged, knowing this was a bridge toward his independence, God willing no unfortunate event would take place.

TWENTY-SEVEN

"Nowhere am I so desperately needed as among a shipload of illogical humans."

– Mr.Spock

June 2011

Bingo's a proud dad and acted as if Gordon had achieved the highest honors. To everyone he met, Bingo rambled on about how Gordon was now taking the public transit on his own. Like Bingo, I also beamed with pride, but I was more cautious of the unforeseen, unfortunate what-ifs parked in the deep recesses of my mind.

Other than his Friday trip to school, Gordon now took the bus for his monthly checkup with his orthodontist. Since the clinic was in another town, that trip required him to use a bus transfer ticket. There was one time when the bus driver of the succeeding bus refused his transfer ticket, but I was glad Gordon could think of an alternative method of payment and gave him the exact fare in cash instead.

Although we celebrated those small steps of success, at the back of our minds, we were still cognizant of his autism diagnosis which came with extra baggage, the outbursts which struck in varying intensities and crept in like thieves in the night, when we least expected them. And there were what we called monster outbursts that jolted us once or twice a year because that was when Gordon lost control.

One humid Saturday afternoon, Patrick, Gordon, and I made a trip to the Oriental grocery store. Upon arrival, we headed to the fruit section. Being a weekend, there were a lot of shoppers that day.

Upon scanning the fruit section, I noticed an oversupply of fruits—pineapples, cantaloupes, and watermelons—in their individual huge boxes measuring three feet high.

"Let's get pineapples," Gordon demanded.

"That's not on our list. I thought we were here for cantaloupes," I reasoned out while checking to see where Patrick was.

Patrick shook his head, not wanting me to give in to Gordon's wishes.

"We still have lots of pineapples at home. Let's get one cantaloupe and some mangoes for our smoothie…" I tried to negotiate with him, but before I could finish my sentence, Gordon growled.

"Hey, hey," he yelled out loud, intending for everyone to hear.

It had not been five minutes since we stepped inside, but Gordon wasted no time and dashed over to the other fruit section, then knocked out a heap of peaches. Convinced that his act was successful, Gordon dismantled the remaining produce.

Patrick and I grabbed his arms.

"Gordon, stop it!" My voice quivered in hysteria. "That's enough."

"Gordon!" Patrick blurted in a much more forceful voice than mine.

On a rampage, Gordon scanned the grocery aisles to inflict more damage. He approached some shoppers and yanked their baskets upside down. They froze, and no one dared to pick up the scattered items on the floor.

"Whoa! What was that all about?" an Oriental guy with a gray beret jerked his head back and yelled at him.

An elderly lady shorter than Gordon, grabbed another man's arm and hid behind him. He must be a stranger to her, but she needed a shield.

In my attempt to stop Gordon from creating more havoc, I clung on to him. My sunglasses slipped, and my sandal strap broke apart. He elbowed me left and right to let go of my grip. I couldn't control Gordon's aggression. I took a break near the fruit stand, physically drained and weighing what my next move would be.

Patrick, who was of the same height as Gordon but weighing thirty pounds less, continued to restrain Gordon, but he was on fire.

People screamed. "Hey, hey!" Terrified shoppers did not make a move and just stayed still.

"God, have mercy," I cried for divine intervention.

Shortly after, four Oriental-looking grocery attendants wearing white lab coats smeared with stains from meat or produce department stood in front of me. I didn't recall them approaching me, but they must have seen me helpless.

In his pleasant voice amidst the crisis mode, one of them asked, "What do you want us to do?"

"Please restrain him," I shot back. My voice was weak, but I kept reiterating my request.

As the four of them carried Gordon like a captive animal, he shook his legs and arms, so he could be freed. "I'm sorry I had to do this, Gordon," I whispered, feeling dejected. Tears streamed down my cheeks. I panned the area, and my heart ached upon witnessing the fearful shoppers and the damage he had done.

"Mom, I'll bring the car to the curb. I'll wait for them there," Patrick raised his voice to be heard as he explained his plan to me.

With my broken sandal, I limped to the exit with my head bowed down, sensing that all eyes were on me like a convicted criminal.

In his quick presence of mind, Patrick turned on the child-proof lock of our four-door Toyota Camry. "You drive, and I'll hold on to Gordon in the rear seat."

Once they successfully shoved Gordon into the car, I sped away. In my haste, I forgot to thank the grocery attendants. Deep inside me, I was in awe of their decency to ask permission in the middle of a crisis. My heartbeat pounded in anger, defeat, powerlessness, and humiliation while filled with gratitude for those attendants, the angels who saved the day.

On our way home, we took the service road instead of the freeway. From the rearview mirror, I could see Patrick struggling to contain his brother. He wrapped his arms around Gordon, but his inner temperature was still at a boiling point. He growled, kicked, and reached for anything to distract my driving. Once freed, he reached for the steering wheel and pulled it to one direction.

Finally, I pulled over to the side of the road. Aware that I was parked illegally, I prayed for the cops to come so they could help me calm Gordon down. Unfortunately, no one arrived.

"Why are we here?" Gordon asked.

"That's because I am not prepared to have an accident, and I don't want anyone to die!" I cried out.

"When are we going home?"

"When you're calm."

"But I am *calm.*" His voice quivered.

"You're NOT. Do not tell me you're calm; I will tell you when you're calm," I sobbed, responding to him as firmly I could while boxing my chest several times to emphasize my point.

My head rested on my two hands clutched to the steering wheel. I felt some tightness on my chest as I continued to weep.

No one moved; no words were exchanged. Gordon watched the cars whizzing by, while Patrick fixed his gaze on the dashboard, Gordon's forbidden area.

After an hour feeling the excruciating summer humidity, I announced, "We're heading home now."

No argument nor response of any sort could be heard.

Upon reaching home, I turned off the engine and faced them. Then, I fixed my gazed at Gordon. "You're staying in the family room, okay?" Seeing sweat beads running down his temples, I reminded him that he needed to cool down.

"Okay," He sounded remorseful in his response.

In the family room, I gave him a lot of water and turned the fan on despite having the central air conditioner already turned on.

"You're staying there until I tell you to move."

I stared down at him lying on the yoga mat on the floor. I felt my heartbeat pounding, and my tears continued to wet my cheeks. I couldn't relate to what I was feeling. All I knew was that Gordon was not in control of what happened, and I felt sorry for him.

Maybe Gordon felt sudden lightheadedness or confusion since we had noticed some outbursts during hot and humid days. We'd been helping him articulate his feelings but like a volcano's molten rock that stays dormant beneath the Earth, extreme heat pushed it up to the surface, seeking out cracks and weaknesses in the mantle. Upon reaching the surface, nothing could stop the now viscous rock from flowing. It would have to erupt as lava, resulting in massive destruction.

***

After a sleepless night, I made it a point to go back to the grocery the following morning. I felt some palpitation as my mind tried to grasp all the chaos Gordon caused. I rehearsed my script to the manager on my way to the grocery store.

I felt people scrutinized me upon my arrival. I wondered if they witnessed what happened yesterday.

"Can I talk to your manager?" I approached the lady at customer service.

"Do you have an appointment?"

"No," I began to stutter. "My son had an outburst here yesterday…"

"Oh, I remember that. Let me call the manager." She was quick to interrupt me with a big smile—a smile I could not interpret. *Did she witness it? Did they have a meeting about it?* Chills ran down my spine as I waited for the manager.

A few minutes later, a young man wearing a clean white lab coat drew near to me.

"Hello," he greeted me with a friendly smile.

I smiled back with some reservation, like a guilty criminal.

"How's your son?"

Before any pleasantries, he wanted to know how my son was? I was not prepared for the friendly reception.

"My son is all right, thank you. I am here to apologize…"

He cut me off. "I am glad to hear about your son."

"I want to pay for the damage…"

"That's all right. No need to pay for anything. We understand." He spoke with an Oriental accent.

"Huh?" My jaw dropped. I was speechless. *They did understand? How could they be understanding of someone responsible for the damage?* "Thank you, thank you, thank you." I made sure he heard my extreme gratitude; it was the least I could do. "One more thing. Thank you to your workers."

"No worries. Take care of your son, okay?"

"Yes, sir. Thank you again." I wondered if he was aware that my son had autism. I wondered if he had a child with autism himself or knew someone who had.

On the way home, unable to hold on to my excitement, I called Bingo from my cell phone, but he was out swimming with the boys. I recollected the different facets of our autism journey.

While I felt guilty for not having lobbied for any autism cause nor volunteering my time to autism events, I was thankful for those who stood out there and had their voices heard for us. Their autism awareness endeavors were palpable.

TWENTY-EIGHT

"Autism is about having a pure heart and being very sensitive. It is about finding a way to survive in an overwhelming, confusing world . . . It is about developing differently, in a different pace and with different leaps."

– Trisha Van Berkel

August 2015

With his keen interests on cars, Gordon was often asked. "When will you start driving?"

"I don't know." His response translated his insecurity of maneuvering a vehicle. At twenty-one years old, he had become aware of his limitations. Being in control of a vehicle may require him to make snap decisions. He remained content being a passenger but happiest as a backseat driver.

If I had to assess Gordon's intellectual capabilities, he had the potential to achieve whatever his heart desired. I recalled that when he was still non-verbal, he was able to determine that milk, among all intake and other stimuli, was the culprit for whatever discomfort he had. In recent years, he had the initiative to take extracurricular lessons, like Kumon and piano. Unfortunately, his heart did not desire to learn other interests, like biology, which he did not see as a practical application at that time. Unlike neuro-typical children who could be forced to test the unknown waters and abide by the curriculum, Gordon adamantly refused. Not to kowtow to his every wish, our focus in preparation for his future wouldn't necessarily be for him to be a scientist or take an office job but for him to have the skills to live independently, the focus of his high school life.

During Gordon's last year of high school, he informed us of his wish to emcee the special education graduation ceremony at the end of the school year. I forced a smile, but deep inside, I tried to assemble the pieces together on how my son's confidence rose.

"For as long as you portray good behavior, with no tantrums, I don't see why they won't allow you to be the emcee." Back when we were running our home program, tangible items and edibles were used as positive reinforcements to elicit appropriate responses and good behavior. The promise of emceeing now served as a positive reinforcement.

To Gordon's delight, he was given the opportunity to host the ceremony. He articulated each word and delivered his lines with conviction. He glanced at each and everyone in the audience, and when his eyes met mine, I felt goosebumps, proud of my son as he was up in the podium as if he were delivering his valedictory address. This reminded me of his toddler days when he would orate like a political candidate running for office, through his babbles. *You've come a long way, my baby.*

I was pumped up while visualizing his bright future. They said that each one of us was the architect of our life. We knew what motivated us to achieve our personal happiness. I wouldn't doubt that Gordon could apply behavior modification to himself to achieve his personal goal. At times, his desired path was not aligned with our dreams for him.

In as much as we wanted him to take up some college courses after finishing high school at twenty-one years old, Gordon had no interest for higher education. He was content to be volunteering his time working with our mechanic in his shop, cleaning the tools and assisting the workers. He had grown to love his job, knowing he got to see cars and vans daily. Occasionally, he got a treat of being in the driver's seat as the car was hoisted up. His *car* knowledge had expanded, no doubt.

It had been two years since Patrick moved to Los Angeles in search of a school offering film music composition. Our home had not been the same since his departure, but we were grateful for technology which allowed us to communicate while we were apart.

We were at the Buffalo airport to catch a flight to Los Angeles. Upon stepping inside the terminal, Gordon was elated since airports were like Disneyland for him. As a collector of inflight magazines, Gordon was familiar with the major airports, including those he had never been to. He studied the area like a supervisor checking on his staff, and when he noticed a painting, he said, "Oh, that's new."

Despite Gordon being in his happiest place, Bingo and I were always on alert mode when we were with him in public. Sometimes, it was when he was very familiar with the area that he pulled a prank, maybe to seek attention or to test the limits of another person.

At the line-up to present our identifications to the TSA agent, he tiptoed and craned his neck to get a feel for the number of passengers before our turn. I wondered if he was antsy when his turn was coming up.

"Are you excited to see your brother?" I started a conversation to distract his attention from whatever his plans were when he faced the agent.

"Ehh," he responded with a funny sound, resembling a sheep's bleat.

"Please remove your sunglasses," I whispered. He ignored me. I let it go. Besides, he looked cool in his dark sunglasses, a baseball cap, in Khaki pants and an Orange Nike dry-fit shirt. Despite the heat, Gordon always traveled in long pants.

"Whatever they ask of you, you need to respond properly, okay?" Bingo reminded Gordon in an authoritative tone as he handed over our passports and boarding passes.

The TSA agent waved at us. *It was our turn.*

Like a soldier, he marched toward the officer. Bingo, who was a few inches taller than Gordon, was right behind him while I stepped aside to be in the agent's line of sight. Gordon handed over his passport and boarding pass before he was asked; he knew the drill.

The agent smiled at him and opened the passport to the picture page.

He offered no smile in return.

"What's your name?" the TSA agent asked.

"Gord," came his curt reply.

I glared at him, hoping he would provide his complete name to the agent.

The agent squinted her eyes.

"Sir, can you please remove your sunglasses?"

"Oh no! I am going to sunny LA." He shook his head. He responded as if reminding the agent that going to LA gave him the right to have his sunglasses on.

A loud thud rocked my chest. I called out to him. "Psst."

Bingo tapped his shoulder and whispered, "Remember, we agreed… do as they say."

Bingo signaled to me that Gordon's defiance might create a scene.

I puckered my lips and nodded, then approached the podium to examine the passport page she was on.

Our whispers were audible to the agent, no doubt. From our eye exchanges, she possibly could feel the tension between us. As I scanned the area, I noticed the line had gotten longer. The terminal seemed to be getting to be more crowded compared to a few minutes ago when we came in. I said a short prayer. *Lord, please put your hands on my son. Don't allow him to make a scene.*

"That's okay." She beamed and glanced up at Bingo and then to me. She must have noticed the Special Olympics button pinned on his cap.

She looked down at the passport picture, then faced Gordon. "I see you have a mole on your left chin," she said while pointing on her left chin like she had a mole in the same position. She flipped the passport page and chuckled, reacting to his signature. "Hmm. *Gord*?"

Her reaction to his signature reminded me of the story Gordon's EA related to us back in grade two. The children were then practicing writing their names in cursive style. When she noticed that he just wrote his name as 'Gord,' she asked, "What happened to the 'on'?" referring to the 'o-n', the last two letters of his name.

"It's off," was Gordon's quick response.

"You're okay, Gord. Step aside while I check your mom and dad." I heard the TSA agent's voice while I blinked my eyes, taking me back to the present.

She winked at us as she gave Gordon back his documents.

What a relief!

By the time we were seated at the pre-departure area, Gordon dropped his bags and was about to explore the airport which was his favorite pastime whenever we traveled.

"Hey, wait a minute, please sit down," Bingo called to him.

He sat beside me, while Bingo was seated on my other side. "I don't like what happened there. Do you understand?"

Gordon didn't reply. Whether he understood or not, all he cared about now was to walk around.

"You have to be serious. Those agents can ban you from flying if you don't respond properly."

"Okay, Dad."

I remained silent while listening to their back and forth exchange. Adding fuel to the conversation might stir Gordon up.

Silence crossed between us.

"Can I go now?" he asked.

We nodded.

He took off in a sprint.

To this day, we make an effort for Gordon not to be given special assistance, so he adjusts to the environment, but we are never prepared for what his behavior would be in public. It is comforting to know that the IATA (International Air Transport Association) has recently introduced the DPNA code (Disabled Passenger, with intellectual and developmental disability, needing assistance). We may use that in the future.

In the meantime, here we were, off to sunny LA, hoping for a pleasant family vacation.

TWENTY-NINE

"Disability doesn't make you exceptional, but questioning what you think you know about it does."

– Stella Young

February 2016

Throughout our years of marriage and our experience living with Gordon's diagnosis, there were still some parenting styles that Bingo and I did not come face-to-face with. Bingo pictured me as the consenting parent which he felt was spoiling Gordon. He did not want me to give in to Gordon's demands, in the same way, I found him too strict with Gordon. Our conflicting styles had to be confusing for

Gordon.

"But remember, if you give him a crack, he'll open it up." Bingo reminded me to always be firm.

At home, that evening, as I approached the powder room, Gordon blocked me. "Don't go in there."

"If the toilet has overflown, it's okay. It's not your fault." I somewhat sensed that was what happened.

Gordon bowed down his head. "It's an accident. Let me go."

I pushed him aside to get through.

"No," He raised his volume a notch while blocking the door to the washroom.

When Bingo came home, he caught us wrestling in the tiled foyer that measured five feet by twelve feet. I stepped back and approached Bingo.

As Bingo removed his shoes and dropped his backpack, I whispered to him about what was going on.

Gordon continued to plant his hands on the doorframe and stared at us. His eyes narrowed as he searched for Bingo's reaction to my news.

"Let me fix it," Bingo declared and attempted to walk over to the powder room.

"NO," he growled, scratching his neck. I sensed something was brewing and approaching boiling temperature. His mouth shut tight, bulging on each cheek.

I signaled to Bingo to let it go for now. He could always check the washroom when Gordon was in bed.

He shook his head, disagreeing with my approach then pushed into Gordon's human blockade, but Gordon exerted full force not to let him in. A vein throbbed in my forehead. I tried not to think about what could become of this. No one gave in to the other.

Aware that Bingo was legally blind without his eyeglasses, Gordon snatched his favorite target and tossed them aside.

"Get my glasses," Bingo yelled at me.

I rushed to pick up his glasses and gave them back to him. While they were in a locked embrace, Gordon kept punching Bingo's back.

"Gordon, stop!" Bingo shouted at him in a forceful, scratchy tone.

I tried to restrain Gordon's hands and feet, but they were much stronger than I could handle.

Bingo did not let go of Gordon. Once he did, we knew he'd go wild, running around and throwing objects that he saw.

That triggered a memory of his tantrum episode last year where he threw my laptop on the floor and shattered the screen. To the repair guy, I declared that the laptop fell by accident.

The repair guy could not believe the damage in my laptop that he wanted me to reconfirm what I said when I brought it in. He informed me that the damage inside could not have happened with an accidental fall. It must have been a deliberate act that caused the damage; my hard drive was irreparable.

As I witnessed the same rage Gordon exhibited last year, their wrestling continued with Gordon attempting to free himself while trying to reach for anything he could throw. He kicked left and right, hitting the walls. Bingo inched them closer to the carpeted staircase. He planned on pinning Gordon down at the bottom of the stairs to grab some air. A few minutes of break was enough to fuel his energy. He was determined to carry on with the wrestling match until Gordon had weakened and tired himself out.

My heart was ripped apart, observing their struggle. *This was not the Gordon I knew. Help me, God.*

As they got closer to the stairway, Gordon lifted his right leg and threw a kick. His kick went through the drywall, creating a hole that measured a foot by a foot.

Bingo's jaw dropped, and his eyes widened at the sight of the hole. His face was livid with anger. He exerted full force to push Gordon down and got him seated at the bottom of the stairs. He was determined not to let go of Gordon nor let Gordon his way.

"Call 9-1-1!" He turned to me and yelled. His eyebrows had merged into a savage line.

I grabbed the cordless phone and punched in the number.

"9-1-1, may I help you?"

"We need help here. My son has autism. My husband and I cannot contain him." My voice quivered with my heart pumping as I spoke to the 911 dispatcher.

"You live in…" The female dispatcher confirmed our address while Bingo kept yelling, "Hurry!"

"The cops are on their way." She was patient and calm in much contrast to the scene there at home.

"By the way, how old is your son?" she asked in her sweet voice.

"Are they coming or not?" Bingo screamed, interrupting my conversation.

I covered the mouthpiece. "They are on their way." I raised my voice to be heard above Bingo's yelling and Gordon's growl. Gordon squirmed to release himself from Bingo.

At past eleven, I checked outside the window, hoping to see the flashing lights in the area. The whole neighborhood was quiet and serene.

"Is that your son growling?" the dispatcher asked.

"Why are you still talking to them?" Bingo blurted out.

I ignored the dispatcher's question. With a hushed tone, I once again informed Bingo that the cops were coming.

After waiting for what seemed like an eternity, two six feet tall cops appeared at our doorstep.

"They're here. Thank you," I ended the call with the 911 dispatcher.

As I escorted the cops inside, I had hoped their authoritative demeanor would prompt Gordon to calm down. Now at his boiling point, anger and frustration flashed over his face. Like a captive octopus, his hands and legs wiggled to be freed.

Immediately, the cops parted them from their locked embrace like what a referee does to boxers competing in a match.

"Do you want us to handcuff him?" One of them faced Bingo while the other cop held on to Gordon.

"Yes," Bingo and I responded quickly and in unison.

One cop handcuffed Gordon with his hands in front of him. He did not resist. Perhaps he was drained by then. With a gentle push, they gestured for Gordon to have him seated and rest on the stairway.

In handcuffs, Gordon, with big tears in his eyes, looked at the cop. A few minutes later, in his remorseful -sounding, calm voice, he said, "When are you going away?"

"Sir, it is our job to ensure safety in the community. When everyone is calm here, when we feel you are all safe, that's when we can leave." The cop clarified to Gordon their purpose of being there, then he added,

"If you continue to display your aggression, we will be forced to remove you from your home, so your mom and dad can have peace."

Tears rolled down my cheeks. I fixed my eyes on my son handcuffed while and seated on the stairs. Deep inside me, I wanted to tell them, *Don't take my baby. He's a good boy.* I sat beside him and ran my fingers on his moist hair, wishing that never happened.

In the meantime, Bingo and the other cop moved to the kitchen, so he could fill in the cops with as much information as necessary about Gordon which they needed to include in Gordon's profile for their database. After Bingo was done, they joined us in the living room.

The cop explained that in the future if they were called again to a scene due to Gordon's rage, they could check their database. He would be handled accordingly based on the information on the database. Gordon seemed to want to rest the right side of his head on the wall, but a hole was in there. He absent-mindedly fiddled with his fingers, giving blank stares. *He must be tired.*

"Are you calm now?" The cop bent down to ask Gordon.

Gordon nodded. The cop removed his handcuffs, then turned to me. "Please get Gordon a glass of water."

I did as I was told.

The cop handed Gordon the glass. "Hey, buddy, drink this and go upstairs. It's already past one in the morning. You should be in bed now."

After he drank the water, I gave him a tight hug before he proceeded upstairs.

As soon as the cops witnessed that everything seemed peaceful, they bid us goodbye and reminded us to call again if any trouble arose.

Once the cops were out of sight, I brought up the topic of having Gordon medicated.

"No. That's not the solution," Bingo said in such an emphatic tone, despite what happened tonight.

Initially, Bingo and I were adamant not to have Gordon medicated. We were afraid of his reliance on the medication, its withdrawal syndromes, and perhaps his moods when medicated. The medications for autism were known to be addicting and could control one's life.

"You know John, see how he is now." He reminded me of our friend's son. It was true; John did not seem to be himself, I recalled.

I agreed with Bingo. I also didn't want him medicated. A cold tremor ran through my body. "What do we do? What if this happens again?"

"He needs to change his ways."

At two in the morning, we were out of fuel to think it through. I tried to grab a wink that night, but the hand of fear clutching at my heart kept me awake while tears wet my cheeks. I longed for Bingo to comfort me with a plan. I guessed he was at a loss for ideas too. Everything that we had done for Gordon just flew out the window. How were we supposed to protect our son during these monster tantrums when he seemed like the enemy, and we couldn't protect ourselves? I buried my face with the comforter, not wanting to deal with what lay ahead.

***

A week later, Gordon and I were in the psychiatrist's office waiting room. Against Bingo's wishes, we were here to ask for a prescription.

Unsure if Gordon really needed to be medicated, our family doctor referred us to Dr. Patel, the psychiatrist we were seeing today.

"Why are we here?" Gordon whispered, uneasiness creeping into his voice. Gordon had worn a long face during our trip here.

I set the magazine I was reading aside, and in my authoritative tone, I said, "I've had it with your tantrums that hurt people and wreck other people's property. You seriously need help."

Head bowed down, Gordon fiddled with his fingers.

I knew he was not in control. Something inside him was causing all the unfortunate acts.

Moments later, we were seated inside Dr. Patel's office. His room layout was like Dr. Pelletier's office, the doctor who diagnosed Gordon more than twenty years ago. Pictures of his family dominated the credenza top.

"Do you hear voices?" Dr. Patel turned to Gordon.

"No." He responded in what seemed to be a remorseful tone.

"Do you know why you're doing it?"

"No."

More questions were asked, and then, he concluded, "He seems okay. I don't see the point of prescribing medication. He looks all right to me."

"But we want an emergency prescription drug to arrest his tantrums," I countered. I knew my son was normal, but when he had these monster outbursts, it could be frightening, and we wanted to avoid anyone getting hurt.

He stroked his gray beard. "Okay, let me write one for you." He scribbled on a prescription pad. "He can take this Ativan, one milligram per day, if you wish, or when you both feel that he is antsy. This medicine should calm him down." He glanced at Gordon and then back at me.

Gordon nodded.

Dr. Patel continued. "This second prescription, also Ativan, has a higher dosage. This is your emergency pill. This is sublingual, under his tongue." He demonstrated to Gordon. "In the middle of the crisis, shove this inside his mouth, and in a minute, he'll be knocked down."

I glanced at Gordon who still exhibited a poker face. How I wished I could bring back his radiant smile.

I realized that when our life skills, a product of our interests, experiences, knowledge, and maturity, are plotted on a graph against the x-axis of time, our life represented in a curvy line, depicting the highs and lows of life. Gordon's life was portrayed like a jagged line graph;, the spread between the highs and lows were steep and abrupt. *For all that he was, and he was not, we loved him as much as we have embraced his autism.*

THIRTY

"If you can dream it, you can do it."

– Walt Disney

August 2018

Since our visit with Dr. Patel two years ago, we had never allowed Gordon to take the medicines regularly. He only took the medicines to arrest upcoming outbursts.

A few months ago, despite knowing that the party we planned to attend would start at six in the evening, he asked, "What time does the party begin?"

We believed this question was meant to rush us, knowing he could not be late and had to be there before dinner was served. Most times, I could relate to Gordon, yet we could hardly rely on Bingo's timeliness especially now that he was very involved with the Special Olympics and other community-related events. He always had last-minute things to attend to. And at times, to prick our patience to the max, Bingo still wanted to check the last few minutes of a basketball game before heading out.

For the party, I tried to remind him. "No need to be on time since this is a social gathering, and there is no specific hour for us to go."

We had been teaching Gordon to be flexible, yet it didn't seem to have convinced him. This time, he did not take any of my excuses and continued asking the same question which revealed his agitation.

"We're leaving in five minutes. Before we leave, you need to take Ativan."

"No, I'm okay," he insisted.

I could feel a storm rising but maintained my composure. "You promised not to have a tantrum anymore," I reminded him. "Here, please take this Ativan." I gave him the low dosage pill to prevent an explosion at the party. I heaved a sigh of relief when he took the pill.

Were it not for the pill, he would have continually asked questions during the drive to the party. "Who will be there? Are we late? Have they started eating?" With that pill, he seemed to have calmed down. By the time we reached the party, his inner temperature had dropped, and he no longer asked annoying questions as he was delighted to see friends.

We continued to help him understand his feelings. It was our hope that someday he'd be able to manage his emotions and take the pill when he needed it. But he seemed to be reminded of the No-to-Drugs campaign he was introduced to while in grade school. He was still reluctant to take the pill on his own and being an advocate to himself was a work in progress.

The Ativan had worked magic in arresting an upcoming outburst and had been a savior. But with the Special Olympics, the program itself was the redeemer.

***

We were here in Antigonish, Nova Scotia, the site of the Special Olympics National Summer Games where Gordon was competing in the track events.

As Bingo and I took our seats at the Keating Millennium Center at Saint Francis Xavier University, I panned the area. It was a mob in here, the blaring sounds, the thunderous crowd, and the blazing lights all around. From all over Canada, the crowd of about fifty thousand waved their provincial flags to show support for their team. A knot formed in my stomach as I anticipated Gordon's reaction to the scene in here. *Sensory overload?*

My thoughts rolled back to two years ago in Newfoundland for his first National Games experience where he participated in the Alpine skiing. Images of Gordon marching in with the Ontario athletes flashed through my mind.

"Hey, Gordon!" Bingo and I jumped up and down, raised our flags, and shouted his name to get his attention. Most of the athletes danced and waved with their flags, marching into the stadium. Gordon looked like a horse with blinders who kept his pace as he clutched the upper arm of the athlete next to him. Inside my winter mittens, my palms were clammy, so I kept my hands in my pockets throughout the duration of the ceremonies.

"Here they come!" Bingo yelled at the top of his lungs. His nudge and deafening voice startled me, and I realized that we were here at the Summer Games Opening Ceremonies.

"Do you see him?" I tiptoed and narrowed my eyes in search of my boy among the throngs of athletes in their red and white Ontario colors. The most populous province in the country, it was no surprise that they came with the largest delegation.

"I see him. There he is." With Bingo's hand on my shoulder, he pointed and bent to my level. "Can you see him? See that blonde lady. That's his track coach. He is to her left."

"Yes, yes, I see him!" I replied to Bingo, then called out to Gordon. "Hi, Gord!"

"Hi, Mom." He seemed to be mouthing those words but the blaring sounds in the air and the distance between us were making his words inaudible at my end. He waved his Ontario flag and lifted his hat to help me spot him.

When all the athletes had settled in their seats and the program was about to begin, I whispered to Bingo, "This is gold." I was over the moon. "Regardless of his performance in this game, he's already a winner." He seemed very proud to be there with his team, representing our community and our province, as proud as I was that he was simply happy to make it there.

Unlike the Ontario Provincial Games, every speech here was delivered in English followed by French. During the French delivery, my thoughts shifted to how Gordon qualified it to the National Games.

Gordon had been with the Oakville track team for close to ten years now. Enthusiastic at first, but after two years of being part of the team, his interest seemed to spiral. He started acting up and disrupting the games at random.

"Can we just pull him out of the team?" Though rare, I was tempted to give up each time he threw those monster outbursts.

"No." Bingo was adamant not to give Gordon a choice. *Bingo was not a quitter.*

"Don't you think you need to be more involved?" I begged him and explained that supporting Gordon on those activities meant more than just financial support. "I help him practice his piano at home, so he's prepared when he goes for his lessons. Can you also train him in track and other sports outside the practice sessions?"

My request paid off. When the Oakville track team coach left his position five years ago, Bingo volunteered to be the head coach which required him to take several Special Olympics accredited courses and other coaching courses. I congratulated him and was thrilled that he had taken the initiative. I hoped he would be closely coaching his son, in addition to coaching their team.

Around the same time when Bingo assumed the coach position, I met the manager for the ski team in our area. She just arrived from Korea where her daughter competed in skiing at the Special Olympics World Winter Games.

I shared with Bingo what Judy told me. "Do you know that this is like the real Olympics? Gordon has a chance to compete at the Special Olympics World Winter Games."

"Maybe if Gordon knows that his efforts will lead to some travel, he will strive harder and show his best behavior." My voice's pitch went up in my excitement.

Bingo didn't appear to share the same enthusiasm as I did and was in deep thought, but little did I know that he was considering my sentiments.

The following winter, we signed Gordon up with the ski team. We dangled the promise of travel for good performance and behavior. As we were not skiers, we relied on his coaches to help him out. To our surprise, not only was he on his best behavior the whole season, he even got the award for the most improved athlete. Two years later, Gordon and another team member represented the province for the National Games.

After dinner one evening, I overheard Gordon approach his dad.

"Can I also go to the National Games for track events?" Fresh from his exhilarating experience from the National Winter Games, the experience must be addictive.

"Look at this." Bingo showed him the roster of athletes. "There are many athletes competing for short distances. Go for the longer distance," Bingo suggested then carried on. "Like fifteen hundred meters, three kilometers, and five K. You think you can handle that?"

"Yes," he responded quickly. Gordon seemed to be seeing his shining star, his guiding star.

"If you really want to advance to the next level, you cannot just be excellent in your performance. You need to demonstrate good behavior at all times, okay?" Bingo reminded him.

When we learned last year that Gordon had advanced to the National Games for track, Bingo posted an announcement on his Facebook public wall. *What a proud dad!*

The pleasant memory was etched in my heart. Back in Antigonish, while watching the performances of the Opening Ceremonies, Bingo nudged me. "What are you smiling about?"

"I just replayed the events as to how Gordon got here." I squeezed his hand and in a hushed tone, congratulated him. "This is all your doing. Thanks to you!"

A puzzled look crossed his face. "What do you mean?"

"Gordon's here because of your efforts; he would not have made it if it weren't for you."

He gave me a tight squeeze. "But it was you who encouraged me to do this, and I have to thank you for that."

I leaned my head on his shoulder, realizing that despite having different views, Bingo had always had my back.

***

The day after the Opening Ceremonies, we caught up with Gordon and asked him about his accommodations.

"I am staying in residence." His eyes lit up as he referred to the university dormitory. Thanks to Special Olympics for the university life experience without fulfilling the academic requirements.

I observed Bingo and Gordon having a conversation with hand gestures, like a professional coach discusses strategies with his athlete.

Worries and stresses stemming from those monstrous outbursts that could have suspended him from participating in these games were muted. I felt every neuron in my brain vibrating in anticipation of a sunny future. *Did he feel ready to take a flight on his own?*

Gordon dreamed of advancing to the World Games. Regardless of the outcome here in the National Games, he had grown to love Special Olympics for all that the program stood for. Quoting its motto, he had learned to be brave in his attempts. The program provided him a positive experience to represent his community, but more importantly, for him, it was to travel with the team and live independently.

If he was not chosen for the World Games, Gordon would continue to pursue his goal. For now, he would treasure his team jackets and wear them with pride.

Nothing could stop my golden boy, my special Olympian. He was going places… and reaching for the stars. He was on top of the world. He was all pumped up and no longer looking at the gray clouds but saw bright colors in his horizon.

THIRTY-ONE

"You're off to Great Places! Today is your day!
Your mountain is waiting, so...get on your way!"

– Dr. Seuss, Oh, the Places

May 2019

To this day, Gordon lived with us and was occupied with his volunteer work with the mechanic and his Special Olympics events. With his activities, I tried to see where I fit in his life. I'd joined them on some hobbies, like running and biking. As I completed this book, Gordon still continued to demonstrate the manifestations of his diagnosis.

He could appear to be quite a conversationalist if any discussion involved his penchant for cars, airplanes, buses, or airports, but of course that limited his audience. There was no doubt he was still quirky and had maintained all his individuality—perhaps one of his strongest assets in some ways—in others, not so much.

A handful of outbursts was still part of every year that we journeyed forward together; they could be a result of his stubbornness or inflexibility as in when he absolutely insisted on having things his way, and his way only. Other times, I wondered if his tantrums were the result of him being provoked or bullied—if we weren't present, we didn't always know the origins. He lived to his namesake, the Gordon train in Thomas the Tank Engine series; he could be brusque but was compassionate.

"You're leaving?" I asked Gordon as he gathered his blue UCLA hat, wallet, and keys. I knew he left early to walk to church, so he could get there half an hour before the mass began, but I continued to ask him that question every week, hoping that one day, he would rather ride with us in the car.

"Bye, Mama." No time for small talk, he planted a kiss on my cheek, donned his hat, then quickly turned around and picked up his pace as if he were running late. He rushed back to me with a Mother's Day card that he personally made. "Happy Mother's Day, Mom." He squeezed me tight.

My heart melted. *To think, I never imagined he would call me Mama,* with an accent on the second syllable. In public, with a volume that sounded like he was speaking through a megaphone, heads turned when he calls me Mama. Annoying at times when he repeatedly uttered 'Mama' until he got my attention, it would always remain the sweetest sound.

As he disappeared from my sight, I proceeded to the kitchen for my morning cup of tea. I opened the cupboard in search of honey, and right before my eyes was Gordon's red Matchbox car. A wide smile played on my lips. *I wondered how long that toy car had been here.*

I picked up the car, recalling how that toy car had mesmerized Gordon, drawing him away from us, siphoning him into his own Neverland. In between chuckles, I realized the power that toy car had on my son, such a positive reinforcement that brought Gordon back to us. That car helped him establish a relationship with his family. Gordon's fascination for those toy cars led him to be captivated by real cars, transportation, and travel; they were always also his key motivators to be on good behavior and work hard to beat his personal best in his Special Olympics activities.

I buried the Matchbox car inside my pocket, a memento I promised to keep.

While stirring my tea, I gazed outside the window as I recalled looking forward to my lilac blooms on

Mother's Day; the elegant pink flowers peeking into my kitchen windows have provided me comfort while its sweet fragrance had given me hope. Gone in the winter, the return of the flowers reminded me how forgiving life could be. *But where were my flowers?* I reckoned I was staring at the mid-section of the tree. I stepped outside, and from my deck, I noticed my tree had grown over thirty feet, surpassing the height of my house. I saw my pink-hued flowers at the tips of their branches above the rooftop. As I let the cool breeze brush against my skin, I realized how my lilac tree's growth paralleled my life as a mother to my boys. Just like that tree now hovering over our home, my 'mothering' role, to provide them security and be their guide to be independent and survive in the real world, had taken on a different dimension. Both Patrick and Gordon were grown up now. *Yes, everything would be all right.*

I examined my kitchen, despite the major renovation ten years ago, the footprints were still the same and the memories remained. We still had the same breakfast table where Gordon would play with his Matchbox toys, where he learned to use utensils, and where we played Candyland and other board games.

I reflected on the basement which served as Gordon's work area, the calendar area, the trampoline area, and the meeting area. *It was no longer my basement.* It was Bingo's basement, or more specifically, it was a Special Olympics basement. There was a nook for Gordon's ski, golf, hockey, and curling equipment. And there was a nook for track and field items, where Bingo was the head coach.

I often thought of Patrick, now living in Los Angeles, as he tried to crack into the field of film music composition. With a keen ear, he had always been into music analysis and composition. Unfortunately, neither Bingo nor I could communicate with him intelligently in his field. We were thrilled for him that he was surrounded by like-minded friends.

"Are you ready?" Bingo popped in and joined me in the kitchen, ready to take me to church. We'd be joining Gordon now seated in the front-most pew.

I put my cup in the sink and grabbed my purse. "Yup. Ready." I looked up to him with a smirk on my face.

He arched his eyebrows.

"Time flies."

We shared a moment of silence in each other's embrace while gazing at the lilacs, truly grateful for each other and for life's blessings.

I had never expected my life to be that way and through our trials and tribulations, we were now closer as a family and always believed that hope prevailed. Life's journey had taught me to embrace Gordon's autism and most of all to love beyond measure.

I closed my eyes, relishing the memory of how it all started, acknowledging that it was the best Mother's Day gift I could ever have.

AFTERWORD

Every now and then, my friends and family connect me with someone who has a family member newly diagnosed with autism in case I can lend a hand or provide guidance.

"What do you suggest they do? Do you have guidelines?"

My heart goes out to this family. How can I help when I am a thousand miles away from the family in need?

In another instance, they have asked me, "Why don't you work directly with children with autism since they will benefit from your knowledge?"

I wish I can. Especially in North America, families will only deal with licensed or certified professionals in the subject. My knowledge is limited only to my personal experience.

In last year's track meet, a parent who has known Gordon since kindergarten came to me. "Look at your son! He has come a long way."

I smiled at him, and while eying Gordon on the sidelines, I beamed with much pride and nodded. Yes, I am proud of him.

"You should write a book." the parent suggested.

"Why?" My forehead creased, reacting to the suggestion. "Gordon has developed no savant or extraordinary abilities popularly attributed to individuals with autism."

"Lots of stories about these amazing individuals have already been written. But the universe is also interested in Gordon's story too," he added.

I mused at that thought. That's true. My son may not have jaw-dropping skills, but his story could be inspirational too.

I never thought I'd be writing our journey. As years passed, the incidence of autism has risen. Each time I mention 'autism,' the stranger I may be conversing with will immediately share his story of someone he knows who is also in the spectrum (autism spectrum disorder) and who may benefit from my guidance and story.

While, thankfully, a plethora of services and resources are now available to the families these days, plus information is now much more accessible, they could sometimes confuse parents who may still be in denial while racing against time to get their child's development back on track.

As I began writing my story, scenes, dialogues, and emotions of those times came flowing into the forefront of my thoughts as if they were stuck in some crevices of my gray matter waiting to be transferred to paper. In situations where I could not connect the scenes, I collaborated with Gordon whose recollection I find reliable. He provided me the dates and some details of the incidents.

The process of sharing my story, which forced me to revisit my deepest emotions, has allowed me to experience some catharsis.

My story is not intended to be a prescribed path to those trekking a similar journey. In sharing my personal experience, I hope the reader will learn from my mistakes and be inspired enough that they see hope in their situation.

Trust your instincts. If you feel something's different, address the issue immediately. Do not wait for services and resources to be available. Remember that the clock of life does not rewind.

If I can impart a lesson learned, partner with credible professionals with strong references and be the strongest advocate for your child, beyond paying the bills and driving him to therapies. Apply the skills learned from the therapy sessions in your home and other settings.

Be your child's best friend. Take time to smell the lilacs in bloom.

ACKNOWLEDGEMENTS

First, my thanks to my editors, Geraldine Zialcita, (www.geraldinesolon.com) and Kimberly Dawn. It has been a pleasant as well as a learning experience. Thank you for the knowledge you've generously shared. I have found a friend in you.

Second, my thanks to my beta readers for their initial reviews and feedback: Vanessa Blackwell, May Mediano, Dr. Randy Prescilla, Ardy Roberto, Dr. Dina Jose, Tina Morrison, Fides Almario, Joy Almario, Mian Gamboa, and Tracie Lindblad.

Third, thanks to my Autism and Special Olympics families, who have traveled with me on this journey. Thank you for lending me your ears and your shoulders I could lean on. To the school staff and therapists and other professionals, thank you for believing in Gordon. You've made a positive difference in his life.

To all the volunteers in our Autism and Special Olympic events, thank you on behalf of the families.

Fourth, my thanks to my families. Our geographical distance has not limited the love and support you've showered on me and my family. Although I have not specifically mentioned her in this book, my special thanks to my mother. Early in my marriage, your words of wisdom to be strong for my family, translating life's bumps into character-building opportunities have resonated in me especially when monkey wrenches were thrown my way. You are like my lilac tree who has comforted me and guided me in my life.

Fifth, my thanks to my son Patrick who has been my ally very early on. I could never fathom the extent of your understanding of your brother's condition but your profound love for him and our family has always been there. My loving thanks to my husband, Bingo, my partner in raising this family. Raised by different parents, we may not see things on the same page and at the same pace. But our love for one another and for our family has allowed us to weather any storm. And thank you for taking care of my lilac tree.

Sixth, thank you, my dearest Gordon. At the time of your birth, I thought I have the exact recipe on how to raise you to what I want you to be. But life didn't turn out that way. You taught me what life is all about. You taught me to celebrate your small successes and appreciate the littlest things in life. Your steadfast devotion to the Catholic faith and especially to Mother Mary has been an inspiration.

And last, I thank God, our Almighty for your guidance for my family and for this opportunity to share my story. Our life is a montage of inspirational memoirs so beautiful they need to be shared to become more meaningful.

I thank you, my reader, for this opportunity to share my story. Please consider leaving a review and rating this book.

RESOURCES

In my library, I referred to these books and websites when I was running our ABA program.

Inspiration Memoirs:

- ➢ Let Me Hear Your Voice – Catherine Maurice
- ➢ Thinking In Pictures – Temple Grandin

Curriculum Resources:

- ➢ Visual Strategies for Improving Communication – Linda A. Hodgdon, M.Ed., CCC-SLP
- ➢ Teaching Reading to Children with Down Syndrome – A Guide for Parents and Teachers – Patricia Logan Oelwein
- ➢ I am Special – Introducing Children and Young People to their Autistic Spectrum Disorder – Peter Vermeulen
- ➢ Classroom Orientation Curriculum – The Eden Institute Foundation, Inc.
- ➢ Symbol Articulation – Lorraine Arcuri

- ➢ A Work in Program – Behavior Management Strategies and a Curriculum for Intensive Behavioral Treatment of Autism – Ron Leaf & John McEachin
- ➢ Teach Me Language: A Language Manual for Children with Autism, Asperger's Syndrome and Related Developmental Disorders – Sabrina Freeman
- ➢ Behavioral Intervention For Young Children with Autism: A Manual for Parents and Professionals - Catherine Maurice, Stephen C. Luce, Gina Green, Gina (Ed.) Green, Stephen C. (Ed.) Luce
- ➢ The New Social Story Book – Carol Gray

Sites

- ➢ Visual Aids
- • https://www.boardmakeronline.com/Login.aspx
- ➢ Home School curriculum
    - • https://a2zhomeschooling.com/materials/curriculum_shop/free_curriculum/free_homeschool_curriculum/
    - • https://allinonehomeschool.com/
    - • http://www.blessedbeyondadoubt.com/free-homeschool-curriculum/

Autism Services

- ➢ Autism Research Institute: https://www.autism.com/
- ➢ Geneva Center for Autism: http://www.autism.net
- ➢ Autism Partnership: https://www.autismpartnership.com/
- ➢ Eden Autism Services: https://edenautism.org/
- ➢ Monarch House: https://www.monarchhouse.ca/oakville-team

Thank you reading my story.

The promise of lilacs starts with one flower, each of us.

May the promise of lilacs give us the courage to
recognize what we are capable of when
facing life's challenges.

May the promise of lilacs empower us to serve.

And may each of our personal stories
serve as an inspiration.

Let's pay it forward. Let your friends know of
The Promise of Lilacs.

Please leave a review. Your review is incredibly helpful
in promoting this author's advocacy.

ABOUT THE AUTHOR

Photo © 2019 Joy Z. Almario

Leah Rivera lives with her husband, Bingo, and son, Gordon, in Ontario, Canada. *The Promise of Lilacs* is her debut memoir. Through her Facebook page, <u>https://www.</u> <u>facebook.com/lilacriv/</u>, she promotes her advocacies on embracing our 'special needs,' our individualities, our uniqueness. She can be reached through this page.

Made in the USA
Lexington, KY
31 October 2019

56301792R00162